Marx's *Capital*

Marx's *Capital*

Third Edition

Ben Fine

Reader in Economics, Birkbeck College,
University of London

MACMILLAN

First edition 1975
Reprinted 1977, 1979, 1981, 1982
Second edition 1984
Reprinted 1987
Third edition 1989

Published by
MACMILLAN EDUCATION LTD
Houndmills, Basingstoke, Hampshire RG21 2XS
and London
Companies and representatives
throughout the world

Typeset by Footnote Graphics, Warminster, Wilts

Printed in Hong Kong

British Library Cataloguing in Publication Data
Fine, Ben
Marx's *Capital*.— 3rd ed.
I. Economics. Marx, Karl, 1818–1883.
Kapital, Das— Critical studies
I. Title
335.4
ISBN 0–333–49456–3 (hardcover)
ISBN 0–333–49457–1 (paperback)

Contents

Acknowledgements

This book is prepared from courses given at Birkbeck College on 'Marxist Economics' and 'The Distribution of Income and Wealth'. I have been influenced by those who taught and attended those courses. Bob Rae and Simon Mohun read earlier versions and have made many suggestions that I have incorporated. I thank those who have given help, but retain sole responsibility for the contents.

B.F.

Preface to the Second Edition

This book was written in the early 1970s and is very much a product of its time. Then, in Britain, an interest in Marx's political economy had begun to be awakened in academic circles. This interest has grown and has been fed by the decline of the world capitalist economy as students of economics have turned away from traditional theory's explanations of the collapse of the post-war 'boom'. Now in the early 1980s we can look upon a decade in which there have been many debates over the issues covered in this book. The results of these debates are necessarily absent from this text. In addition, the book was written when the author himself was still relatively new to Marx's critique of political economy. For these reasons, if the book were to be written now, it would be different. There would be differences in argument and differences in emphasis.

Nevertheless the book does have certain advantages, because of rather than despite its particular history. It is an introduction or entrance to Marx's *Capital* and is not the final word but rather a starting-point from which the reader can understand Marx's text and the capitalist economy. Because it was constrained to be short the arguments are condensed but remain simple, without the complications introduced by controversial debate. Although, in retrospect, embarrassing mistakes were made from place to place, I was generally surprised by the extent to which the text has survived the passage of even such a short time. This is due mainly to the fact that I attempted to reproduce Marx's ideas from *Capital* rather than to develop a few ideas into a 'Marxist economics'.

I have, however, changed the text in a number of places. These are generally marginal changes, the major exceptions being the attempt to avoid sexist formulations in language (which suggested a world of men alone) and the last chapter on the world economy which has been replaced by an article, slightly amended, which first appeared in *World Marxist Review* in January 1980. Some errors still remain in the book but they have quite deliberately been left uncorrected for the sake of simplicity. This is perhaps most serious in the case of Marx's theory of agricultural rent. However, I have laid out my own views on this subject elsewhere: 'On Marx's Theory of Agricultural Rent', *Economy and Society* (August 1979) and the debate with Michael Ball in the same journal (August 1980). Otherwise a more sophisticated and developed treatment of the issues covered here and the debates to which they have given rise is to be found in the book, written jointly with Laurence Harris, *Rereading 'Capital'* (Macmillan, 1979). I have taken up in more detail the criticism of bourgeois economic theory and its relation to ideology in *Economic Theory and Ideology* (Edward Arnold, 1980) and in *Theories of the Capitalist Economy* (Edward Arnold, 1982).

Finally, I would like to extend my thanks to Piet Steenbakkers whose preparations for the Dutch edition of this book led to the revisions. His influence is to be found on almost every page.

December 1983   BEN FINE

Preface to the Third Edition

The third edition has been substantially revised and extended. While some chapters have remained pretty much as before, some have been dropped altogether, some have been cut, some revised, and others have been extended. In addition, new chapters have been written to cover at greater length economic reproduction, the transformation problem, the law of the tendency of the rate of profit to fall, interest-bearing capital and rent theory. This has meant drawing upon articles from *Science and Society* of 1985/6 ('Banking Capital and the Theory of Interest') and from *Economy and Society* of 1979 ('On Marx's Theory of Agricultural Rent'). One of the effects of the revisions is to confine the book to coverage of Marx's theory as presented in *Capital*.

The new structure of the book is as follows. After a brief discussion of methodology in Chapter 1, Chapters 2 and 3 consider the labour theory of value (as does Chapter 11 in terms of the transformation problem). Chapters 4 and 5 examine production and accumulation, and the coverage of Volume I of *Capital* is concluded by examining primitive accumulation. Chapters 7 and 8 discuss the circulation of capital, and Chapters 9 and 10 are devoted to crisis theory. Chapters 12 and 13 focus on the theories of interest-bearing capital and rent respectively.

As before, the intention has been to present Marx's arguments as clearly but also as concisely as possible. These two objectives do not always coincide, with the result that some of the material will require careful reading, particularly the later chapters. One way of distinguishing Marx's view has been to contrast it with other schools of economic thought. This method has been employed from time to time but, hopefully, not at the expense of excluding the reader not specialised in economics. For ease of reading, footnotes and references have again been omitted. Those interested in a more scholarly text are referred to the contributions listed in the Prefaces.

Finally, I would like to thank and to encourage those who continue to study and teach Marxist economics seriously, during a period, in Britain at least, when it has been hardest to do so.

December 1988 BEN FINE

MARX TO ENGELS

'The best points in my book are: (1) the *double character of labour*, according to whether it is expressed in use value or exchange value... (2) the treatment of *surplus value independently of its particular* forms as profit, interest, ground rent, etc.'

Selected Correspondence, Letter 99 (Lawrence & Wishart, London, 1934).

MARX TO J. WEYDEMEYER

'And now to myself, no credit is due to me for discovering the existence of classes in modern society or the struggle between them. Long before the bourgeois historians had described the historical development of this class struggle and bourgeois economists the economic anatomy of the classes. What I did that was new was to prove: (1) that the *existence of classes* is only bound up with *particular historical phases in the development of production*, (2) that the class struggle necessarily leads to *the dictatorship of the proletariat*, (3) that this dictatorship itself only constitutes the transition to the *abolition of all classes* and to a *classless society*.'

Marx and Engels, *Selected Works* (Lawrence & Wishart, London, 1968) p. 679.

1

Method

The materialist conception of history

Marx's methodology can usefully be described as one of abstraction and successive approximation. By 'abstraction' we mean extracting the essentials, not being purely theoretical or divorced from reality. The process of successive approximation does not really mean moving closer to a better 'solution', but the building of explanations of phenomena on the structure of the essentials. If these explanations are impossible in terms of modification or extension of the first stage of abstract analysis, this implies the essentials themselves are inadequate and need to be changed.

As a methodology this is hardly controversial and does not need much elaboration. What is important is the content given to the methodology that is Marx's method, and the intended scope of its application. In his pursuit of the revolutionary transformation of society it was Marx's purpose to uncover the general process of historical change, to apply this understanding to particular types of societies, and finally to make concrete studies of particular historical situations. To understand how he did this it is convenient to study what Lenin describes as the three component parts of Marxism, which were the culmination of early nineteenth-century intellectual development – German philosophy, French socialism and British political economy. In this section we

1

discover how Marx's philosophy and socialism led to his understanding of the general process of historical change. His application of this and his exploitation of British political economy in the study of capitalist society is the subject of the remainder of the book.

Marx was born in Germany in 1818 and began an early university career studying law. His interest quickly turned to philosophy, which at that time was dominated by Hegel and his disciples. They were idealists and believed that the study of man's consciousness was the key to the understanding of society. (This was their abstraction. Just as science leads to the development of technology, so intellectual progress is the basis for the advance of government, culture and the other forms of social life.) Historically, Man progressed towards the Idea, the perfection of institutions, culture, religion, and hence society. History was a dramatic stage on which institutions and ideas battled for hegemony. For Hegel this conflict was ever present, the existing state of affairs always contained a tension with what it was becoming. Each stage of development contained the seeds of transformation to a higher stage. Each stage was an advance on those that had preceded it, but it absorbed elements from them. This process of change, in which new ideas did not so much defeat the old as resolve conflicts within them, Hegel called the *dialectic*.

Hegel died in 1831. When Marx was still a young man at university, two opposed groups of Hegelians, Young and Old (radical and reactionary), both claimed to be Hegel's legitimate successors. The Old Hegelians believed that Prussian absolute monarchy, religion, and society represented the triumphant achievement of the Idea in its dialectical progress. In contrast the Young Hegelians, dangerously anti-religious, believed that intellectual development had far to advance. This set the stage for a battle between the two schools, each side believing a victory heralded the progress of German society. Marx having observed the absurdity, poverty and degradation of much of German life, identified himself initially with the Young Hegelians. For the participants the great debate, conducted as philosophy, transcended politics. The struggles of the real world paled to insignificance against the advance to be made in ideas.

Marx's sympathy for the Young Hegelians was extremely short-lived, largely because of the influence on him of Feuerbach, who was a materialist. By this we do not mean he was crudely interested in his own welfare, being in fact sacked from a university position for his views. He believed that far from human consciousness dominating life and existence, it was human needs which determined consciousness. In *The Essence of Christianity* Feuerbach mounted a simple but brilliant polemic against religion. Humans needed God because religion satisfied an emotional need. To satisfy this need, Man had projected the best qualities on to a God figure, worshipping what had been made to the extent that God had assumed an independent existence in human consciousness. To regain humanity humans needed to substitute the love of each other for the love of God.

Marx was immediately struck by this insight. Initially he criticised Feuerbach for seeing people as individuals struggling to fulfil human nature, rather than as social beings. However he soon moved beyond Feuerbach's rather crude materialism. He did this in two different ways. First, he extended Feuerbach's materialist philosophy to all dominant ideas prevailing in society, this is to say to ideology and people's conception of society as a whole. Secondly, he extended Feuerbach's ideas to history. Feuerbach's analysis had been entirely ahistorical and non-dialetical. Man satisfied a 'material' emotional need through religion. But the origin of that need remained unexplained, even if we could explain the idea by the need. Marx saw the solution to this problem in material conditions, in other words the way in which production was organised. This was the abstraction that he made. In contrast to the Hegelian dialectical progress of ideas, Marx took the contradiction between the forces of production and the relations of production (described below) as the motive force of historical change. Human consciousness was critical in Marx's thought, but it could only be understood in relation to historical, social and material circumstances.

In 1845–6 when he was writing *The German Ideology* with Engels and the *Theses on Feuerbach*, Marx had already begun to be influenced by the ideas of the French socialists. These ideas, fostered by the heritage of the French Revolution and the failure of emerging bourgeois society to realise the demands of '*liberté, egalité et fraternité*', were dominated by class politics and often included belief in the necessity and possibility of revolutionary seizure of power. Socialism has many different meanings to different people and political movements. For Marx, socialism is more than an idealised reorganisation of society and is certainly not a programme for reforms for capitalism. He believed that a socialist society, in which classes would eventually disappear, would be based on the productive power developed by capitalism, organised according to a plan formed by the full decision-making participation of working people.

However, central to Marx's socialism is the notion that it is the proletariat which is going to make the ultimate change in the order of material life. Socialism is the identification with this class and with its struggles. Marx had little time for utopian socialists or others (except to condemn them vehemently) who envisaged or idealised a new structure for society without seeing the means for its attainment: revolution by the proletariat. This perspective gave him the key to all history, most simply stated in *The Communist Manifesto*, as 'The history of all hitherto existing society is the history of class struggles.' How easy to identify the proletariat's task of overthrowing capitalist society once history was seen as the outcome of class struggle! Conversely the class antagonisms that Marx perceived in society in his own time cannot have failed to suggest to him the application of class analysis to previous epochs.

Marx's method for studying the general process of historical change was essentially complete. He called it the materialist conception of history and never used the terms 'historical' or 'dialectical' materialism. He gives an excellent description of this method in the *Preface to a Contribution to a Critique of Political Economy*. We now tie these remarks together.

In organising production people enter into relations with each other – as capitalist or wage-earner, as slave or master, or as lord or serf. These relations exist independently of their choice even though they have been historically made in the course of historical development. The relations of production specific to a particular mode of production, for example capitalism or feudalism, are best studied as class relations in all but the most simple societies. They are the basis on which the whole of society is constructed with limited variability. Definite forms of political, legal and intellectual life correspond to definite modes of production. Just as freedom to buy and sell are key legal characteristics of capitalist society, so divine or feudal obligation are the legal foundations of feudalism.

Reflection on an individual's situation and on society will have little influence on the pattern of choices available. Patterns of life are most severely constrained and defined by existing social conditions, in particular the places to be filled in the process of production. In addition a self-justifying super-structure of political, legal, intellectual and distributional forms has also already been established, and these in general blinker and discourage all but the most conventional views of society, whether by physical force or force of habit. In entering the relations of production people inevitably find in social existence, in practical day-to-day life, the unconscious rationale for the system. The serf feels bound by loyalty to master and king. The wage-earner has freedom to sell labour. There can be struggle for higher wages, but this does not question the wage system.

This all demonstrates the stability existing in a given mode of production. The crucial questions are how can that stability be threatened and how can the will to change the system of production be generated. Society can be seen in a new light, and not as immortal, only when the conditions of production are disrupted. When the duke is unable to fulfil his feudal obligation or the worker unable to sell labour-power, then feudalism or capitalism may be challenged. This occurs historically when the forces of production, crudely the technological ability to produce, are held back by the relations of production. The forces of production tend to be dynamic, changing frequently and placing great strains on the relations of production which are sluggish and inflexible. Manufacturing is impossible under feudal relations, as is efficiency and profit maximising. Attempts to accommodate the forces of production within the existing relations bring a breakdown in those relations, and with this down falls the old superstructure of ideology, and so on. These changes do not come about overnight but are contained in a century of progress and stumbling. The development of the relations of production depends upon the outcome of class struggle. The ruling class of any mode of production always resists the advance of the conditions favourable to the class that is to be dominant in the new society. Working people will be torn between two competing systems of oppression, until under capitalism they constitute the emerging ruling class.

Marx's economics

Given his conception of history, it was natural for Marx to turn his study to economics in analysing capitalism. To do this he immersed himself in British political economy, in particular developing the labour theory of value from the value theory of Smith and Ricardo. For Marx, however, it was insufficient to base the source of value in exchange on labour-time of production as had Ricardo. This takes for granted the existence of exchange, prices and commodities. That commodities are more valuable because they embody more labour, begs the question of why there are commodities at all, let alone whether it is a relevant abstraction to assume they exchange at their labour-time of production. This anticipates the following chapter, but it illustrates a key feature of his method and a common criticism by Marx of other writers. Marx found other economists not so much wrong as inadequate. He was interested in probing beneath the appearance of society to the reality below. This meant taking nothing for granted, leaving no important phenomena of society unexplained. What economists tend to assume as timeless features of humans and societies, Marx was determined to root out and understand.

Marx did take for granted, as part of human nature, the need to produce and consume. The way in which production was organised had to be revealed, and the dependence of other social relations on this explained first structurally and then historically. For example Marx castigated the utilitarians for their assumption that certain characteristics of human behaviour, like greed, were permanent features of 'human nature', when they were characteristics generated in individuals by particular societies. To distinguish people's possible relations with the physical world from those induced with it and other people, Marx spoke of Nature and nature respectively. It was part of Marx's task as well as his method to explain human nature, and throughout this book we shall attempt to understand how people view economic relations and behave accordingly.

Clearly Marx's economics, in contrast to much contemporary orthodox economics, is a social science in that it concerns itself with the relations that people set between themselves, rather than with the technical relationships between things and with the art of economising. Marx was not interested then in constructing a price theory, a set of efficiency criteria, or a series of welfare propositions. These would depend upon assuming a limited potential for society to change and standards of welfare rooted within the framework of that society.

This is not to suggest that Marxism contains no normative content. Rather, like any theory interpretative of society and its people and their social relations, it is an amalgam of positive and normative judgements, the disentangling of which would be an endless task. Indeed the separation of positive and normative theory so popular in modern economics is an impossible one for Marx beyond the trivial, whether purely empirical, or wildly utopian. On the one hand statistical relationships, even if value free, can provide no theory of causation without interpretation of the society from which they are drawn. On the other hand the application and meaningfulness of normative propositions depend upon their possible fulfilment. Investigating this requires the unravelling of the social, political and economic ties that bind societies. Economists who maintain a distinction between positive and normative inevitably take for granted those features of capitalist society that Marx felt it necessary to explain: the private ownership of the means of production, their operation for and distribution by exchange, with remuneration involving the economic categories of prices, profits and wages.

2

Commodity Production

The labour theory of value

In analysing a mode of production, for example capitalism, Marx's starting point is always production. In any society the object of production is use-values, that is to say useful things such as food, clothing, houses, and immaterial products like plumbers', GPs' or nurses' services. Thus the production of use-values can be taken for granted, just as production itself can be. In addition, at the first level of abstraction, it is unnecessary to explain the distribution of use-values in production, that is, the relative quantities of each product produced. This would depend upon a whole host of influences, for example ideology, technology, and the distribution of income, which could only be studied themselves after the basic relations of production had been uncovered. Contrast this with modern economics with its neutral government and given utility functions and factor endowments.

One fundamental feature of capitalism is that it is a highly developed system of commodity production. Following Adam Smith, Marx distinguishes use-value from exchange-value: usefulness, which cannot be quantified, from the ability to exchange with other commodities, which can be quantified. Every commodity has a use-value, but not every use-value is a commodity, for use-values, which are either

8

freely available or are not exchanged, have no exchange-value (for example air and production for personal use).

Marx sees exchange-value as embodying a numerical equivalence relationship between objects, at first in the abstract. This relationship has to satisfy certain properties, which become familiar to us at school and in daily life. If x exchanges for y ($x \sim y$ say), then $2x \sim 2y$. If, in addition, $u \sim v$, then (u and x) $\sim$ (v and y), and so on.

But there are an unlimited number of relationships between objects satisfying these properties, for example weight, volume. The question Marx wanted to answer is what is the determinant of the relationship of exchange of commodities. What is the thing common to two commodities that causes them to be equivalents in exchange? In the case of weight or volume, equivalence is due to a physical or natural property, namely mass and size respectively. However, although every commodity is characterised by its particular physical properties which give it its use-value, its exchange-value has no systematic relation to these properties. Even the most useful things, air, sun and water, often have little or no exchange-value. What creates the relationship of exchange is not a physical relationship but an historically specific social one, the relationship between commodities as the products of human labour. This will be clarified below.

For Marx it is axiomatic that throughout history people have lived by their labour. Further, beyond the most simple societies, some had always lived without working, by the labour of others. However, this appropriation of one person's labour by another took different forms and was justified in different ways in different societies. Under feudalism the mode of distribution of produce was often by direct appropriation justified by feudal or even divine right. Under capitalism produce is distributed by the free exchange of commodities, and so the free exchange of the products of labour. How this freedom could bring about an appropriation of the labour of one class by another will be discussed in the next chapter. For the moment we are only interested in the nature of the exchange relationship.

We have seen that a commodity necessarily contains a use-value, but a use-value is not a commodity unless it

embodies a labour-cost (and is exchanged). Thus, the property that all commodities have in common, that creates the
relationship of exchange, is that they are the product of
labour. This is the basis of the labour theory of value, and it
embodies a social relationship which can easily be theoretic-
ally quantified by analysing exchange from the viewpoint of
the labour-time necessary to produce commodities: for
example, the amount of labour-time required to bake a loaf
of bread. The labour theory of value is not a metaphysical
notion, despite the impossibility of empirically calculating
values, for it expresses definite facts about material life. For
the same reason, nor is it a purely ethical theory, despite its
view of Man as producer rather than abstainer, sinner or
factor of production, as Man is viewed in traditional theories
(for which see pages 25–6).

Marx realised that under capitalism, where exchange of
commodities is pervasive, production is for exchange and
not for immediate use. Capitalism is a system in which the
aim of production is social use-values – use-values for others
unknown because of the anonymity of the market. The
production of social use-values and exchange is intimately
linked. But just as products embody social use-values, so
they are created by social labour in the abstract. Thus, what
exchange represents is the exchange of the products of
individual concrete labour treated as abstract social labour.
Exchange is not interested in quality (type) of labour but
only in quantity, and that quantity is of abstract social
labour. In exchange, the point is not whether the labour-
time was expended by a baker or a tailoress, but *if* a certain
amount of labour-time has been expended.

This is not to suggest that commodities do exchange at
their values, the labour-time necessary to produce them
taking account both of direct (living) labour inputs and
indirect (dead) labour inputs (the labour-time necessary to
produce produced means of production, i.e. raw materials
and fixed machinery). Thus, for scarce goods, market prices
above the amount of socially necessary labour-time can be
obtained, and when goods are in excess supply the prices will
be lower. Market prices will be modified by differing capital–
labour ratios, scarcities, skills, monopolies, and tastes.

These influences have been the prime object of study of orthodox economists since the neoclassical revolution of the 1870s, with little advance being made on Adam Smith's ideas of the 1770s. They were not ignored by Marx, but they are irrelevant, as we shall see, for uncovering the social relations of production specific to capitalism. If this cannot be done on the assumption that commodities exchange at their values, it certainly cannot be done in the more complicated case when they do not. Throughout, unless otherwise stated, we shall assume that commodities exchange at their values. This is not to be interpreted as a fully fledged price theory.

Thus, capitalism, as general commodity production, is characterised by the production of social use-values and hence the exchange of the products of individual concrete labour expressed, in exchange, as abstract social labour. Marx's labour theory of value incorporates a social relation: the exchange of the products of individual concrete labour. As a price theory it is at best a poor approximation, but the important point is that the relationship between exchange, prices and values is not purely quantitive, it reflects definite social relations of production and distribution. It is these that must be understood. It is worth noting that a labour theory of value only occurred and could only occur historically, when commodity production and exchange of commodities had developed sufficiently. Certainly changing ideas reflected changing relations of distribution, but it is the capitalist relations of production in which we are interested. We can now turn to these having understood the nature of commodity exchange.

Labour and labour-power

In the exchange of commodities we have seen that the exchange of different types of labour products takes place. This could occur without capitalism, if independent artisans exchanged their products. Marx called such a situation simple commodity production. It is more a logical possibility than ever an historically realised dominant mode of production.

What characterises capitalism is not just the exchange of the
different products of the different labourers, but the purchase
and sale of the labourer's ability to work. To distinguish the
labourer's work from the ability or capacity to work, Marx
called the former labour but the latter labour-power. Under
capitalism labour-power becomes a commodity, the pur-
chaser is the capitalist, the seller is the labourer. The price of
labour-power is the wage. The labourer sells labour-power
to the capitalist, who determines how that labour-power
should be exercised as labour to produce particular commodities. As a commodity, labour-power must have a
use-value, and this is that it is the creator of use-values. This
is a property independent of the particular society in which
production takes place. However, under capitalism, use-
values are produced in the form of commodities and, as
such, embody abstract labour-time or value. Thus, labour-
power as a commodity also has the use-value that it is the
source of value when exercised as labour. In this it is unique
(note that use-values, but not values, can also be created
naturally). Labour-power, the creator of specific use-values
in commodity form and hence the creator of value, is the
commodity that must be bought by the capitalist. Then the
capitalist, not the labourer or producer, owns and sells the
produced use-values as commodities.

The labourer is not therefore a slave in the conventional
sense of the word and sold like other commodities, but owns
and sells labour-power. Also the length of time for which the
sale is made is often very short. Yet in many other respects
the labourer is like a slave. There is little or no control over
the labour process or product. There is the freedom to
refuse to sell labour-power, but this is a limited freedom, the
alternative in the limit being starvation or social degradation. One could as well argue that a slave could refuse to
work. For this reason the labourer under capitalism is best
described as a wage-slave.

On the other side is the capitalist who controls the
labourer and the product by the command of wage payments
and the ownership of the labourers' tools and raw materials
or means of production. This is the key to the property
relations specific to capitalism. For it is the capitalist class's

monopoly of the means of production which ties the labourer to wage-slavery. If the labourer owned or was entitled to use the means of production, there would hardly be a need to sell labour-power rather than the product on the market, given the profit made by the capitalist. Now we see that the labour theory of value not only captures the distributional relationship of the exchange of labour products, but also embodies the more fundamental relations of production specific to capitalism, once the distinction between labour and labour-power is drawn. The social exchange of labour-power, in addition to the exchange of the products of labour, presupposes the monopoly of the means of production on the one hand and the existence of a class of wage-labourers on the other. Naturally it is precisely this distinction which is never drawn in orthodox economics with its 'neutral' terminology of factor inputs and outputs, which suggests that the labour and capital inputs have an equal position in the production process.

The fetishism of commodities

Marx was able to see that in the exchange of produced use-values the exchange of labour products took place, but to many of his contemporary economists and to nearly all subsequent ones, this relationship between workers and their labour remains merely a relationship between things, that is to say 1 coat = 2 pairs of shoes. Thus, whilst capitalism organises production in definite social relationships between producers, these relationships are expressed and appear as relationships between things. This way of presenting economic relations is further mystified when money enters and everything is analysed in terms of price. Marx called such a perspective on the capitalist world the fetishism of commodities. It is most apparent in modern economics, where even labour-power is treated as an input or factor like any other. Factor rewards are seen first and foremost as due to the physical properties of the factors, as if land or machinery could produce rent or profit rather than people existing together in particular relationships in particular societies.

Marx drew the brilliant parallel between commodity fetishism and feudal religious devotion. God is humanity's own creation. Under feudalism, human relationships with God concealed and justified the actual relationships to fellow beings, an absurd bond of exploitation and slavery as it appears to the *bourgeois* mind. Capitalism, however, has its own God and bible. The relationship of exchange between things is also created by people, concealing the true relationship of exploitation and justifying this by the religious doctrine of freedom of exchange.

Commodity fetishism characterises people's outlook in general, worker and capitalist alike, and this can be made the basis of a theory of alienation. Not only is the worker divorced from the control of the product and the process of producing it, but the view of this situation is distorted. The capitalist is subject to the control of exchange and profit-making. For both, it appears that things exert this control, and not the social relations of production peculiar to capitalism. For example, the loss of employment or bankruptcy with subsequent poverty may be blamed on a thing or impersonal force, for example the unfortunate breakdown of a machine.

Marx's concept of commodity fetishism forges a link with his earlier work of 1844. Then, whilst breaking with Hegelian idealism and adopting a materialist philosophy, he developed a theory of alienation. This concentrated on the individual's relationship to physical and mental activity, fellow beings and consciousness of these processes.

In *Capital*, after extensive economic study, Marx is able to make explicit the social coercive forces exerted by capitalist society on the individual. These can be the compulsion of profitability and wage slavery or the more subtle distortions by which these forces are ideologically justified: abstinence, the work ethic, freedom of exchange, and commodity fetishism. Unlike other theories of alienation, a Marxist theory places the individual in a class position and analyses perception of that position. Each is not seen, in the first instance, as a powerless individual in an unexplained 'system' of irrationality, impersonality, inequality, authoritarianism, bureaucracy or whatever. These phenomena have their own character and function in capitalist society at a particular time. They can only be understood as a whole or in relation to individuals against the perspective of the needs of capital at that time. The basic such need for capital is to create profits, to be examined in Chapter 4 after a more formal analysis of the labour theory of value.

3

The Labour Theory of Value: A Formal Analysis

It has become conventional to present the labour theory of value in algebraic terms. We follow this fashion below, although we observe at the outset that this tends to diminish the qualitative nature of Marx's theory of value – the aspect which so markedly distinguishes his contribution from those of other adherents to the labour theory of value, such as Ricardo.

Suppose a unit of output (corn, say) is produced by l units of labour using (sowing) A units of the good as an input. For those versed in matrix algebra and input-output analysis, A and l can be interpreted respectively as the input matrix and the vector of labour inputs for a number of different goods.

The labour theory of value has been traditionally concerned with the definition of value in terms of the quantity of labour embodied in a unit of each of the goods produced. There are two different ways of working this out. Whilst each gives an identical algebraic answer, each is open to a differing conceptual interpretation.

The first way, what might be called the accounting method, is based on the idea that the same amount of labour that goes into the production process must also come out at the end. If the value of the commodity is λ then the amount that goes in is $\lambda A + l$. The amount λA is called the dead labour going into the commodity, since it is the labour that has already been spent in producing the input A. In later chapters this will be seen to correspond to constant capital, c. The new labour being added, l, is called living labour. We assume throught that $A < 1$, for otherwise the economy sows more than it reaps (or that the economy is productive in the case of matrix A).

The amount of labour that comes out is simply λ, the value of one unit of the commodity. Accordingly,

$$\lambda A + l = \lambda$$

From this, it follows that

$$\lambda = l / (1 - A)$$

(or $\lambda = l (I - A)^{-1}$ in matrix notation).

Conceptually, important assumptions have been made in this derivation. It has been presumed, from the three terms in the original equation, that dead labour (λA), living labour (l) and the labour in new commodities (λ) are all measurable against each other. From a Marxist point of view, such an assumption has to be justified, not by reference to a mental exercise as carried out above, but by reference to the socially specific conditions in which production takes place. This, as argued in the previous chapter, is justified in Marx's analysis by reference to a commodity-producing society in which different labours are brought into equivalence with each other through the act of exchange.

Significantly, the derivation above need make no mention of commodity production. As a formal exercise, it could apply to any human act requiring (labour) time and resources. It would of necessity leave unanswered the questions of what labours are to count and for how much. (Should we, for example, count the time taken in going to and from work, in preparing for work, etc?)

The second way of calculating value is by what might be termed the hypothetical-historical method, since it works out how much labour has been carried out in the past to produce the commodity. In the present, the labour used is the living labour l. But this has been used in conjunction with the corn sown, A. This was produced in the previous period by use of A^2 units of corn and lA units of living labour (living then, dead now), since if 1 unit of corn is produced by A and l, A units will be produced by A^2 and lA. But the A^2 units of corn had to be produced and this must have taken A^3 units of corn and lA^2 units of labour. If we carry on like this into the indefinite past, then it follows that:

$$\lambda = l + lA + lA^2 + lA^3 + lA^4 + \ldots$$

This can be understood as the sum of the labour taken to produce the corn over each period from the present back into the indefinite past.

$$\lambda = l(1 + A + A^2 + A^3 + A^4 + \ldots)$$

The expression inside the bracket is an infinite geometric progression which sums to $1/(1-A)$, or $(I - A)^{-1}$ for the matrix analysis, giving the same algebraic answer as before for value. But the conceptual interpretation must be rather different, since now it is being presumed, in the context of an unchanging technology over time, that labours expended at any point in time are measurable against each other. It is surely the case that such an assumption is either totally unacceptable without the sort of justification given by Marx, so that value exists and is analysable within a commodity-producing society because equivalencies are established between different types of labour (dead or alive); or value becomes a mere formal definition whose applicability is severely constrained by the assumptions that make it operative. Unfortunately, too many interpreters, and especially critics of Marx, have taken the latter alternative and correctly rejected what they incorrectly thought to be Marx's theory of value.

In later chapters we will see how important this question of equivalence between labour-times becomes when technology is changing through the accumulation process. Meanwhile, consider a classic example of the misuse of the labour theory of value as exposed in terms of the discussion above.

In *The Wealth of Nations*, Adam Smith concerned himself historically with the question of under what conditions the labour theory of value would hold. By this is meant under what conditions commodities would exchange at their values. His answer was that this would be so only in the state that he called the rude society. Here hunters would spend time hunting deer and beaver and take one and two hours per animal respectively. Accordingly, Smith argues, two deer would exchange for one leaves (in inverse proportion to the time taken to catch them).

As a mental exercise this appears to be faultless, but the fatal flaw for deer and beaver alike is that neither is a commodity, and there would be no systematic exchange in the society under consideration. Hunters would simply go out and catch whatever they required. In this way we can see that Smith has been constructing a labour theory of value in much the same way as in the algebraic exercises presented earlier. Value is taken to be a mental construct independent of the society under consideration. Not surprisingly, Smith rejects the labour theory of value for societies in which there is exchange (on the grounds that commodities do not exchange at their values). For Marx it is the other way about. Commodity-producing societies are precisely the ones in which value, as defined by labour-time, exists and becomes an essential analytical category despite, or even because, commodities do not exchange at their values. The relationship between values and prices is explored in Chapter 11.

4

Capital and Exploitation

Exchange

We have emphasised that the production of use-values in commodity form tends to conceal the social relationships of production between workers and their labour by concentrating attention on exchange relationships between things. Nevertheless, as simple commodity production demonstrates logically and a history of trade demonstrates in reality, exchange itself can exist without capitalism. It is when labour-power itself becomes a commodity that the seeds of capitalism are sown. In this chapter, by examining exchange from the perspectives of a worker (or more generally a consumer) and then a capitalist, we will see why this must be so.

Essential to exchange, beyond simple bartering, is money. The functions of money have been well explored. It is a unit of account, a means of payment, and a store of value. We rely upon the first function throughout this book. As a means of payment it mediates the process of exchange. (Note that, at any one time, this use conflicts with its use as a store of value, and this is important in crises. For the moment we are interested in exchange only.)

Consider an individual who owns some commodity but would prefer to exchange it for another. First the commodity must be exchanged for money. We represent this by $C-M$.

Secondly the money obtained is exchanged for the desired commodity, $M-C$. Commodities are advanced for money in order to purchase different commodities, and this can be represented by $C-M-C$, the circulation of commodities. We denote the two extremes of the circulation by C because they are in commodity form and they have the same value, not because they are the same thing. Indeed they cannot be the same thing, otherwise the whole purpose of the exchange is defeated. Given no cheating, there is no gain or loss of value in any of the transactions, each of which, in principle, could be reversed. This is summarised in Figure 4.1.

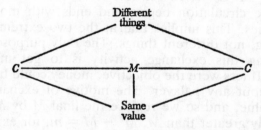

Figure 4.1 Simple commodity exchange – selling in order to buy

Typically, under capitalism, this simple commodity exchange could start with a labourer. The only commodity available to sell is labour-power, and this is a means of consumption, by its exchange for wages (M) and eventually wage-goods (C). Alternatively the exchange could be undertaken by a capitalist. The value of produced commodities is realised on the market, and can then be used to purchase raw materials and labour-power to renew production or buy consumption goods.

Capital

A capitalist starts with money. With this commodities of a special type, means of production, or inputs, including labour-power ($M-C$) are purchased. A necessary condition for this is the willingness on the part of the labourer to sell labour-power. This willingness, an exercise of the 'freedom' of exchange, is forced on the labourer. Selling labour-power becomes, on the one hand, a condition of work. It is the only access to the means of production monopolised by capitalists. On the other hand it is a condition of consumption, as it is the only commodity that labour is able to sell.

Having gathered together inputs the capitalist organises production and sells the resulting ouput. In this is eventually retrieved the money form $C-M$. The dash here conceals the intervention of production in the transformation of the inputs into money, and this will be discussed in Chapter 7. For the moment, we can represent a capitalist's exchange activity by $M-C-M$. In contrast to simple commodity exchange the circulation begins and ends with money, not commodities. This implies that at the two extremes is the same thing, not different things. The only purpose then in undertaking this exchange activity is to get more, not different. If less were the objective, money could be thrown away without any palaver. The motive of exchange is to expand value, and so we replace the final M by M'. M' is numerically greater than M, $M' - M = m$, for example.

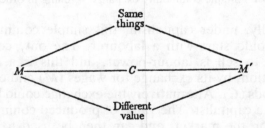

Figure 4.2 Capitalist exchange – buying in order to sell dearer (contrast with Figure 4.1

Money only acts as capital when it is used to generate more money. The purpose and nature of capital is to act as self-expanding value. An understanding of this allows capital to be distinguished from the various forms it assumes and the functions undertaken by those forms, whether it be as money, commodity or factor input. Each of these is capital only in so far as it contributes directly toward the self-expansion of value. As such it can function as capital, as well as performing its function as means of payment, depository of exchange-value, or means of production.

We have characterised capital as self-expanding value by examining the exchange activity of an industrial capitalist. There are other forms of capital, though, namely merchant capital and loan capital. Both of these also expand value by buying (merchandise or bonds rather than means of production) in order to sell dearer. Both appear historically before industrial capital. It was Marx's insight to reverse historical appearance and analyse capitalism in its pure form, without the complication of mercantilism or usury. By assuming that no value is created in exchange, Marx was able to show that capitalism can rely upon the exchange of equal values. Its secrets must lie in production and not in exchange. We follow his example and accommodate other forms of capital in exchange in Chapter 12. This abstraction is borne out historically by the relative increase of industrial capital, but it in no way relegates finance or commerce to the insignificant.

Exploitation

Most economists might find this characterisation of capital as self-expanding value uncontroversial, even if a little odd and unnecessary. In Figure 4.2 we see that although M and M' have different values, M and C have the same value. This implies that in the movement $C-M'$, extra value has been created. Marx called this added value 'surplus value'; numerically it equals m and this is the difference between the values of inputs and outputs. It is not the existence of surplus value (profit in its money form) that is controversial, but the explanation of its source. We have already located the source of surplus in production by assuming that exchange does not create any value. This means that among the commodities (C) purchased by the capitalist there must be one or more that creates in production more value than it costs. However, we have already established the labour theory of value as the appropriate analytical tool to reflect the social exchange of commodities that characterises capitalist production. The search for the commodities that produce surplus value is now limited to those that contribute more labour-time (value) to outputs during production than they cost to produce as inputs. This leaves just one candidate – labour-power.

First, let us consider the other inputs. Whilst they contribute value to output as a result of the labour-time that has been necessary to produce them in the past, the quantity of value (labour-time) that they add to output is no more nor less than that past labour-time, that is to say their own value or cost. Non-labour inputs cannot transfer more value to outputs than they cost as inputs. Now consider labour-power. Its value is the cost of its purchase, which, in real terms, is no more nor less than the labour-time necessary to produce the real wage, a subsistence bundle of commodities. The value it creates in production is the quantity of labour-time exercised in return for that wage. Unlike the other inputs, there is no reason why the contribution made by labour-power to the value of output should equal the cost of labour-power. Indeed it can only be because the value of labour-power is less than labour-time contributed that surplus value is created. From a purely logical point of view the wage could exceed labour-time contributed, giving 'negative surplus value'. If this happened one would find that there would be an abrupt halt in the use of money as capital, as it could no longer function as self-expanding value.

We have demonstrated by using labour-time as our unit of account that, for capital to fulfil its role as self-expanding value, the value contributed by a labourer to output exceeds the remuneration received for the labour-power. The labour theory of value is forced upon us because we are analysing commodity exchange. Capitalism, under which not only the products of labour but also labour-power become a commodity, must produce surplus value, and this must be created by the excess of labour-time over the value of labour-power. Labour-power not only creates use-values; when exercised as labour it also creates value and surplus value. The strength of this argument is seen by its brief comparison with alternative theories of value.

Theories of abstinence, waiting, or intertemporal preference depend upon the sacrifice by capitalists of present consumption as the source of profits. Nobody could deny that these 'sacrifices' (usually made in luxurious comfort) are a condition of profit, but like thousands of other conditions they are not a cause of profits. People without capital could abstain, wait, and make intertemporal choices until they were blue in the face without creating profits for themselves. It is not abstinence that creates capital, but capital that requires abstinence. Waiting has existed in all societies, it is even to be found among squirrels. Similar remarks apply to viewing risk as a source of profit. It must always be borne in mind that it is not things, abstract or otherwise, that create economic categories, for example profits or wages, but definite social relations between people.

Marginal productivity theories explain the increase in value between C and M' by the purely technically determined contributions of labour (wage cost) and capital goods (rent and profit considered as cost of machinery used, etc.) to output (total costs). Such a theory can contain no social content, except to reflect *bourgeois* values. Labour is treated on a par with other *things*. Factors of production have existed in all societies, but the same cannot be said of profits, wages, rents or even prices. No distinction can be drawn between simple commodity exchange and capitalism, because labour-power and labour are not distinguished, there being no interest in the social organisation of production but only in quantities of means of production.

All value, including surplus value, is created by labour then, and all surplus value is brought about by the exploitation of immediate, direct or living labour. Suppose a labourer works a ten-hour day, but that the necessary labour-time to produce the wage is five hours. Then for five hours each day work is 'free' for the capitalist. In this case the rate of exploitation defined as the ratio of surplus to necessary labour-time is 5/5 equals 1 or 100 per cent. Note that this definition could be applied to modes of production other than capitalism, for example feudalism with feudal dues or slavery. In these last two cases the fact of exploitation is apparent; it is only under capitalism that exploitation in production is veiled by the freedom of exchange. Marx referred to the rate of surplus value when being specific about exploitation under capitalism.

Denote surplus labour-time by s, and necessary labour time by v, called variable capital. Together s and v make up what we called living labour, l, in the previous chapter:

$$s + v = l$$

The rate of exploitation, $e = s/v$. v is called variable capital because the amount of value that will be added by it is not fixed in advance but depends upon the amount of surplus labour that can be extracted. It is variable in contrast to constant capital (c). This is not capital fixed in production (a factory) but raw materials and wear and tear on fixed capital, in so far as it is consumed during the period of production (for example, one year). Given a machine that lasts ten years and costs £100, constant capital can be taken to be £10 per annum. It is constant capital, because its value does not vary during production but is preserved in output by the worker's labour, a service unwittingly performed for the capitalist. c and v are both capital because they represent value, in money form, advanced by capitalists. The value λ of any one commodity is made up of constant and variable capital and surplus value, $\lambda = c + v + s$. Its cost is $c + v$, leaving the surplus value (s) to form profit in money form.

The total amount of surplus value produced for a capitalist depends directly on the rate of exploitation and the total amount of labour employed. The latter can be increased by accumulation (see Chapter 5). Assume that real wages remain unchanged. The rate of exploitation can be increased in two ways, and attempts to increase it will be made – for the nature of capital as self-expanding value imposes an important qualitative objective on its agents: profit maximisation, or at least that the growth of profitability should take a high priority.

Firstly, e can be increased through what Marx called the production of absolute surplus value. On the basis of existing technology – that is, the values of commodities remain the same – the simplest way to do this is through extension

Worker produces more value

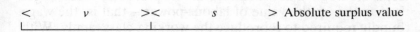

Commodities have same values

Figure 4.3 Production of absolute surplus value

of the working day. If, for the example given above, the working day is increased to eleven hours, then the rate of exploitation will rise to 6/5 or 120 per cent. The production of absolute surplus value is illustrated in Figure 4.3.

However, there are other ways of increasing the production of absolute surplus value, as this merely requires that more labour be performed in exchange for the value of labour power, v. If, for example, work became more intense during a given working day, then absolute surplus value would be increased. This can be done through making work continuous without breaks either of limited duration or even for rest and refreshment. A mechancial way of bringing this about is through the use of conveyors on the production line which would dictate the pace of work (although such work practices are often also associated with technical advance, which would change values and increase profitability other than through absolute surplus value alone).

Alternatively, the pace of work within a given working day could be obtained through a crudely applied discipline. There may be constant supervision by middle management and penalties and rewards, even dismissal in the former instance. But more informal methods might also be employed. A system of wages based on piece-rates, for example, encourages the worker to set a high pace of work, whilst a premium for overtime is an inducement to work beyond normal hours (without necessarily eliminating the production of extra surplus value, for otherwise there would be no profit involved for the capitalist).

Yet another way of producing absolute surplus value is the

extension of work to the whole of the working-class family. It appears that children, wife and husband all receive a separate wage. But the structural role played by those wages is to make up the value of labour-power – that is, the wage bundle required to reproduce the working-class family. With the extension of waged work to the whole family, it is possible through labour market pressure that more labour is provided for little or no increase in the value of wages as a whole.

There are severe limits in the extent to which capitalism can depend upon the production of absolute surplus value. Quite apart from the natural limits of twenty-four hours in the day, the physical and moral welfare and the resistance of the working class are barriers to absolute surplus value. Nevertheless it is always important in the early phases of capitalist development, and at any time it is a remedy for low profitability – if the medicine can be administered.

The development of capitalism brings the production of relative surplus value as the dominant method of increasing e. This occurs through technological change, whereby the value of labour-power (v) is reduced by reducing the labour-time of production of the wage bundle. In this case the working day remains at ten hours, but v falls to, for example, four hours, leaving a surplus value of six hours, with $e = 6/4$ or 150 per cent. There are many mechanisms for doing this, co-operation and finer division of labour, use of machinery and factories, increasing the pace of work, and scientific discovery. The production of relative surplus value is illustrated in Figure 4.4, and this should be compared with Figure 4.3.

Marx attaches great importance to the analysis of the way in which production develops under capitalism. He devotes considerable attention not only to the power relations between workers and capitalists but also to the more specific question of the technical relations under which production takes place. In particular, for developed capitalism, he argues that the factory system predominates. Within the factory, the production of relative surplus value would be pursued through the introduction of machinery.

Machinery would result in rising productivity by allowing

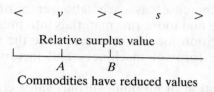

Worker produces same value

$$< \quad v \quad > < \quad s \quad >$$

Relative surplus value

A B

Commodities have reduced values

Figure 4.4 Production of relative surplus value

a greater amount of raw materials to be worked up into final products with a given amount of labour time. Initially, the physical power of the worker will be replaced by the power of machinery; then the tools in the hands of the worker will be incorporated into the machinery, so that ultimately the worker is increasingly dispensed with by the machinery and becomes its appendage – to feed and watch over it.

On the other hand, this process increases the intensity of work in a way which differs from that experienced under the production of absolute surplus value, for now machinery combines together what were previously a number of separate tasks. This has contradictory effects on the role of the working class as producers. They are deskilled by the machinery that displaces them and simplifies their tasks at work, but they are also required to command new skills as a number of simplified tasks are combined. Similarly, the physical burden of work is both lightened by the power of machinery but also increased through the pace and intensity of work.

To a large extent, this analysis presupposes a given set of products and production processes which are systematically transformed through the increasing use of machinery. Marx does not neglect, indeed he emphasises, the role of science and technology in bring forth innovation in both products and processes. But quite clearly such developments cannot be the subject of a general theory of capitalist production since their extent and rhythm is contingent upon non-economic factors such as the progress of scientific discovery.

Nevertheless, Marx does conclude that the factory system will lead to a massive increase in the ratio of physical capital to labour, what he termed the technical composition of capital. This follows on immediately as a consequence of productivity increase, as each labourer must on average work up more and more raw materials into final products. It is also a condition for this to occur, since the mass of fixed capital in the form of machinery and factories must also increase.

The production of absolute surplus value could be based on the grim determination of an individual capitalist using lock-outs and dismissals, although class collaboration and state intervention are rarely found wanting when required. In contrast, assuming that real wages remain unchanged, production of relative surplus value eventually depends critically upon all capitalists, since none alone produces the commodities needed to produce the entire wage bundle, making payment in kind. In particular it depends upon other capitalists' accumulation inducing the technical change that brings the value of labour-power down. Why this accumulation takes place and some of its consequences are the subject of Chapter 5.

5

Accumulation

The coercive force of competition

In a system of commodity production it is logically possible
that the supply and demand for each product would exactly
match, with each commodity exchanging at its individual
value (the labour-time of production whether it be by the
most or least efficient method). Capitalism, however, is
dominated by commodity production, and the extension of
the market ensures that prices for identical products do not
diverge. Even if supply and demand match now, the only
way that the owner of a commodity can ensure that it sells at
(or above) its individual value is by ensuring that this value is
at (or below) the market evaluation, by expanding only one
and a half hours of labour-time on a shirt with a market
evaluation of two hours. Competition is created between
producers in the market. The reaction to this by an independent self-employed artisan, who had survived the vagaries of
the market, would be to modify output either in quantity or
type. These options are also open to the capitalist, but
neither is likely to be as effective for the purpose of
expanding value as joining in the battle of competition.
Marx stressed that this battle is fought by the cheapening of
commodities through reducing their value, that is to say the
labour-time necessary for their production. This is achieved
by technological advance, achieving lower cost per product

31

unit by using the most productive technology, continued renewal of production methods and producing in larger units (scale advantages), which requires accumulation of capital.

Accumulation, from the perspective of an individual capitalist, can be either aggressive or defensive. An attempt can be made to steal an advantage over rivals by reducing the labour-time of production through accumulation, or, being assured that aggressive accumulation will be undertaken by a rival, a response in kind is necessary to defend existing capital. But each capitalist is in the same boat. Socially a situation of competitive accumulation exists, the condition of survival being to take part. In brief, capital as self-expanding value creates competition which is fought by accumulation. The need to accumulate is felt by each individual capitalist as an external coercive force. Accumulate or die; there are few exceptions. Other modes of production and independent artisans are destroyed by the sweeping advance of productivity and the iron rule of market evaluation.

This sort of argument is usually more readily accepted in other social contexts, for example competitive nuclear armament (even though national hostilities may remain unexplained). Consider also the sales side of competition. Capitalists, whatever their beliefs about the benefits of advertising *per se*, have no doubts about its necessity for their own survival. The net effect of competitive advertising may be to leave market shares unimpaired, just as the effect of competitive accumulation may not change profit shares. Nevertheless the need to advertise becomes a coercive force exerted on capitalists independently of their will as soon as advertising becomes historically established. Not surprisingly the capitalists' will or belief soon turns to support these actions, as they sing the virtues not only of their product but also of their informational services.

This ideological twist of self-justification occurs in the case of accumulation also. Marx argued that the emergence of capitalism brought with it the necessity of accumulation and an ideology to support and justify that need. He did not view the rise of capitalism as the history of the development of a protestant, thrift or acquisitive ethic as did Weber, but he considered the historical needs of capital as the force behind a changing ideology. This is not to deny that individual rates of accumulation depend upon individual subjective factors, but these do not exist in limbo. Indeed these factors are liable to increase the rate of accumulation, as under capitalism wealth, as measured by exchange value, also becomes the measure (and means) of social status.

The process of competition

An immediate consequence of competition is the tendency for rates of profit and wages to be equalised as economic agents seek maximum exchange value for their commodities on the market. As an abstraction we assume that equalisation does occur, this depending upon perfect mobility of capital and labour.

Competition is fought by the returns to scale gained by accumulation. These returns have been well documented by many economists, but they are usually seen as technological relationships. However, they have profound implications for the organisation of social and individual life. The factory system emerges, creating new conditions of labour. Inside each factory machinery exerts its own discipline, and the co-operation of labour contrasts sharply with its finer division accompanying specialisation. Outside the factory towns become rapidly growing industrial centres disrupting every relation between town and country, the latter's life itself becoming revolutionised by this and capitalist methods of production.

A capitalist's ability to compete is limited by the potential to accumulate. Sources of accumulation are twofold. First, profits may be re-invested, amassing capital over time. Marx called this the process of concentration. Second, a capitalist can borrow and merge, gathering together the existing resources of capitalist production. This Marx called the process of centralisation. Concentration is a slow process diluted by inheritance, but centralisation through the lever of a highly developed credit mechanism accomplishes in the twinkling of an eye what would take concentration a hundred years to achieve.

As the individual capitalist accumulates, what is true of each is true of capital as a whole. This is reflected in the social accumulation of capital, the reproduction of capital and its relations of production on an expanded scale, increase of the proletariat and development of the forces of production. But the individual capitalist's solution to competition is not reproduced on a social scale. (Think of the arms race and competitive advertising.) Accumulation is also undertaken by competitors so that competition itself is reproduced. Competition causes accumulation, accumulation creates competition. Those who fall behind in the accumulation process are destroyed. First it is independent artisans who are swept aside, but later capital turns on itself, big capital destroying little capital as centralisation, credit and concentration amass more and more capital in fewer hands. Accumulation brings frequent technological revolution as the instrument of leaps in productivity. These developments of capital cannot be isolated from the development of the struggle between the two great classes, proletariat and *bourgeoisie*, to which we now turn.

The development of the proletariat

Let us suppose that as capital accumulates the ratio (c/v) remains unchanged. This does not imply that there is no technological advance, because the relative quantity of physical output may have increased. Provided that the real wage remains unchanged, it follows that the employment of labour increases, since an increased total capital is divided in the same proportions between constant and variable capital.

However, it is unrealistic to expect that the labour supply can be increased indefinitely without an increase in wages. Thus in so far as the wage rate increases faster than productivity in the wage-goods sector there will be a squeeze on profitability. Whilst we have not discussed the quantitative determination of the rate of accumulation it is clear that it will tend to be reduced by a squeeze on profitability. Certainly there will be no accumulation of capital when wages approach such a level that the production of any surplus value at all is threatened. Yet as accumulation slackens so does the demand for labour, and the upward pressure on the wage rate is reduced as labour's power diminishes with unemployment. Profitability is restored, and with it accumulation, and the cycle repeats itself. This argument has to be qualified should the ratio (c/v) change. We consider this in Chapter 10.

This is how Marx characterised the decennial business cycles observed by early nineteenth-century economists. He linked them to the synchronised renewal of fixed capital and the volatility of commercial credit. In contrast to others he explained fluctuations in employment by fluctuations in the rate of accumulation and its effects on wages and profitability. He considered absurd the Malthusian doctrine of alternating decimation and stimulation of the size of the proletariat by sexual reproduction in response to wages below and then above subsistence. This could hardly explain ten-year cycles. Marx was also the first economist not to be spellbound by the idea of decreasing returns in agricultural production. In contrast he stressed the productivity of capital.

Described in these aggregate terms, economic activity, generated by changes in the rate of accumulation, appears to fluctuate smoothly. Nothing could be further from the truth. The overall picture may conceal enormous variations between sectors of production and geographical regions within a capitalist economy. Marx highlighted this by pointing to the constant tendency of capital to expel living labour from the production of a given mass of commodities. This tendency exists as long as technological advance is at all labour-saving. But Marx argued that technical change would not only save living labour absolutely, but also relative to other means of production. As previously argued, this was because increases in productivity require increases in the technical composition of capital (amount of machinery and raw materials per worker as a physical, non-value relationship), since they are achieved by the economies of scale due to factories and machinery. Thus there will be an increase in the amount of machinery per worker associated with an increase in the scale of production. These in themselves increase the technical composition, but they also speed up the process of production. A labourer turns over a given mass of raw materials in a shorter time, reducing the amount of labour contained in a commodity relative to the other inputs.

The expulsion of living labour from the production of a given mass of commodities may be accompanied by an overall expansion in employment with the aggregate expansion of production. Competitive accumulation, however, proceeds in an unco-ordinated fashion. Across sectors and regions outputs and employment will not expand in balanced proportions. With the technological changes there will now be a shortage, now an excess of labour available, but with the expulsion of living labour from the labour process, there will be a continuous flow of labour into unemployment to form a surplus population, or what Marx called an industrial reserve army of unemployed. Among these will be created a layer of permanently unemployed, condemned to relative pauperisation by their unsuitability for capitalist employment, whether it be because of age, discrimination, or physical or mental disability. The greater is the reserve army relative to employment, the greater is the competition for employment and the lower will be wages. But the greater is the absolute size of the reserve army and its layer of permanently unemployed, the greater is the extension of poverty and misery. Marx singled out this feature of capitalism as the absolute general law of capitalist accumulation.

So far we have analysed the requirements that capital accumulation places on the proletariat – a constant disruption of individual and social life. Particular changes may be forced by political, economic and legal coercion, or induced through the market by changes in wages. The particular method chosen and the outcome will depend upon the strength of organisation behind the two classes. Under capitalism, as for any mode of production, the ruling class finds its strength in all superstructural phenomena, the state, the law, and not least the political and ideological consciousness generated by the notions of economic and political freedom. In addition the *bourgeoisie*'s strength increases as accumulation is accompanied by greater centralisation.

However, at the same time as capital is centralised, so are masses of workers concentrated together in the organisation of production. Their social organisation in production encourages their political and economic organisation, and with it their influence on superstructural phenomena like the state. As misery and oppression are extended with unemployment, so the strength, organisation and discipline of the proletariat grow with the development of its material conditions. Capitalism fulfils the positive role of developing society's productive potential. Yet at the same time it develops both the agent of its own destruction – an organised proletariat – and the rationale for that destruction: the socialisation of consumption to be accomplished by a socially co-ordinated plan harnessing that productive potential. The proletariat accomplishes its historical role, expropriation of the *bourgeoisie* when *bourgeois* society can no longer provide the conditions that both capital and labour require of it. This does not necessarily occur during an economic crisis. For whilst this is associated with reduced profits, high unemployment, and so downward pressures on wages, a recession is also a time when the working class tends to be weakened. In addition, changes within a mode of production, let alone the transition from one to another, cannot simply be read off from economic conditions alone but is also highly dependent on political and ideological conditions. These, together with the labour movement's economic position, tend to be at their strongest when conditions are prosperous. So the relationship between economic analysis and revolution is not only complex, but is dependent upon other influences as well.

6

The Transition to Capitalism

So far we have characterised capitalism as a mode of production and revealed the logic and consequences of its compulsion toward accumulation. This provides us with a framework in which the development of capitalism as the world's dominant mode of production can be understood. For, having uncovered the relations of production specific to capitalism, we can isolate the forces behind their creation from the mass of phenomena peculiar to *bourgeois* revolution. Marx devoted a large section of Volume I of *Capital* to the task of interpreting the genesis of British capitalism, and this must stand as a major application and confirmation of his conception of historical change. Here we can only outline the theoretical aspects of his work, and refer the reader to *Capital* and later Marxists for more concrete study of the causes of the nature, timing and location of the first industrial revolution.

The essential feature of capitalism is the existence of labour-power as a commodity. A necessary condition for this is the separation of labour from ownership or claim to the means of production. The labourer has to depend upon somebody else to provide these, otherwise the product of the day's labour rather than the labouring day would be sold. On the other side of the coin must be the capitalist with

38

money to advance to purchase labour-power and maintain ownership of the other means of production. The establishment of these social relations of production out of feudalist ones holds the key to the birth of capitalism.

In any society beyond the most primitive there will be saving of produce to form means of production for the future, whether it be hunting weapon, corn seed, animal stock or machinery. Capitalism is distinguished by the rate of increase of saving that is made. Marx found it commonplace, once capitalism had been established, for other economists to place its creation at the hands of self-sacrificing and energetic entrepreneurs, ploughing back their meagre profits into their businesses. More recently development economists have tended to consider the fact that too small a part of income is saved (low rates of saving) as a major barrier to industrialisation. Marx poured scorn on such a limited outlook. Capitalism was founded on the forcible separation of labour from the existing means of production, and not the capitalisation of surplus value that characterises developed capitalism. This entailed the conversion of the use of existing means of production, including labour-power, into their social use in capitalistic organisation. This does not require in the first instance any additional accumulation of means of production or even their more efficient use, just their operation according to new relations. Once this has occurred the process of competitive accumulation gathers its own momentum.

Since the dominant sector of production in the pre-capitalist era was agriculture, this sector contained the source of a class of 'free' wage-labourers. The secret of primitive or early accumulation of capital lay, then, in the history of the expropriation of the agricultural population from the land, the destruction of the right or custom of individual independent cultivation (even if feudal dues need be paid). This could be undertaken on an individual basis by landowners responding to the growing claims of exchange criteria, but required the power of the state to make any headway in a violent and violently resisted process. The state's intervention, representing the interests of an emerging *bourgeoisie*, was twofold. First, enclosure movements dispossessed the peasantry of both common and individual land usage. The landless labourer was created. Second, wage legislation and systems of social security, culminating in the Poor Law of 1834, forced long hours and discipline on the landless labourer. This turned the landless into a wage labourer, creating the source of absolute surplus value.

Here we cannot stress too strongly Marx's emphasis on the conversion of the method of use of the existing means of production rather than their explosive accumulation. No doubt technical progress and reorganisation of production contributed to the rise in agricultural output that was to feed an industrial proletariat. Few labourers felt the gain of this increased output, and for those that did, it must have paled into insignificance against the deterioration of working conditions and the destruction of a way of life. Illustrative of this is the necessity of physical force in the creation of the proletariat rather than the smooth operation of market forces. This contrasts with most present-day labour relations, where the dull compulsion of economic relations and their development through tradition, education and habit induces the working class to look upon the conditions of the capitalist mode of production as self-evident. Force is rarely used now, because labour is effectively tied to capital and appears as if it always has been and always will be.

The capitalist first appears as a farmer and is long in embryonic form. In Britain capitalists came to the fore through the coincidence of favourable economic conditions – the discovery and hoarding of precious metals, and low rent and wages. The industrial capitalist's genesis was less protracted, developing more out of artisans and guilds and depending upon the absorption of the labourers that capitalistic farming pushed out. Simultaneously a domestic market was created for the produce of industrial capital by the ending of the peasantry's essentially self-sufficient livelihood. Previously they had been able to serve their own needs, means of production being made available according to feudal custom. With the advent of capitalism, money to advance to purchase means of production is required to pursue independent production. Thus it is not necessarily the efficiency of capital that destroys household production:

indeed, household production still persisted in sweat shops. The technical methods of production remain unchanged, but the partial control of output and access to inputs is lost to the producers.

This extremely brief account explains the origins of the capitalist relations of production. By the seventeenth century the first enclosure movement (another was to follow in the eighteenth century) had been completed, creating a landless labouring class. In the eighteenth century the use of the national debt, the taxation system, the protectionist system, and the exploitation of colonies to accumulate wealth had reached its climax. The combination of labour and wealth in capitalist relations accompanied these processes, with the nineteenth century heralding the technological innovation and growth of industrial society.

It is as well to recognise, however, that the creation of capitalism in Britain has been rather different than elsewhere. The forcible dispossession of the peasantry from the land was more extensive than in the rest of Europe. For this reason a much larger proportion of the population was transformed into wage labourers. At the same time this was done through the creation of a system of large-landed property, so that a relatively small number of 'aristocrats' came to hold the vast majority of privately owned land. Elsewhere in Europe the peasantry, or sections of it, proved better able to defend itself by taking possession of the land in smaller parcels, thereby making themselves independent of wage-labour.

The significance of these differences persist to the present day, with Britain's agriculture continuing to benefit from larger farms and Britain's working population containing many fewer employees (and self-employed) in the agricultural sector. However, whilst Marx's analysis of primitive accumulation focused on Britain, and to that extent dealt with something of an exception, his analysis of the formation of the class of wage labourers out of the agricultural population remains an important starting point.

7

The Circuit of Industrial Capital

The money circuit of capital

Volume I of *Capital*, which we have now briefly covered, is self-contained and gives primarily a general analysis of capitalism and its process of development. The other two volumes of *Capital* are devoted both to elaborating and extending this general analysis. For this reason it is appropriate that the beginning of Volume II of *Capital* should analyse the circuit of industrial capital. This is because it can form the basis for understanding a whole series of capitalist phenomena – distribution, commercial, interest-bearing and fixed capital, the turnover of capital, productive and unproductive labour, and crises – as well as providing an economic structure in which the social relations of production analysed in Volume I can be set.

The money circuit of capital is an expansion of the characterisation of capital as self-expanding value (see Chapter 4), taking explicit account of the process of production.

$$M-C\ldots P\ldots C'-M'$$

Throughout this chapter we assume, unless otherwise indicated, that we are dealing with a single capitalist, who

42

exchanges commodities at their values without fear or hindrance. The capitalist starts with money (M) and purchases commodity inputs (C), including labour-power (LP) and other means of production (MP). It should be realised that it is not money as means of payment or in its function as money which allows it to operate as capital, but the separation in ownership of labour-power from the means of production, a definite social and class relation of production. This can be stressed by explicitly separating the means of production in the circuit

$$M - C <^{LP}_{MP} \ldots$$

Labour and raw materials are brought together by the action of money, but it is not money that has made them separate.

On purchase the inputs (C) form productive capital (P). Production proceeds as labour-power is exercised on the other means of production, and the result is commodity outputs (C'). C and C' are linked to P by dots to indicate that production has intervened in the process of exchange between the purchase of inputs (C) and sale of outputs (C'). See Figure 7.1 overleaf. The commodities produced with P are denoted by C', because they contain surplus value (ΔC) over and above C, $C' = C + \Delta C$. The surplus value $s = \Delta C$, created in production by the purchase of labour-power at a value below labour-time, makes its first appearance in commodity not money form. It corresponds to a definite quantity of the outputs (C'), which can be seen to have an excess value over that of the inputs (C). Because surplus value makes its first appearance immediately after production it is easy to credit its creation to the productivity of factor inputs and ignore the necessary condition of its existence, $M - C <^{LP}_{MP}$. It is difficult to credit surplus value to the excess of actual over necessary labour-time, because its appearance is delayed until after production has taken place, whereas the free exchange of labour-power for its value takes place before production.

The produced value (and surplus value) C' is now converted into money form M' by its sale on the market or realisation. Here $M' = M + m = C' = C + \Delta C$, where $m =$

$\Delta C = s$. With M the capitalist can renew the circuit of capital, and m can be used to embark upon its own circuit of capital or be spent on consumption.

The circuit as a whole

The circuit of industrial capital is best represented by a circular flow diagram. As the circuit repeats itself, surplus value (m) is thrown off. This shows that capital as self-expanding value embraces not only definite social relations of production, but is also a circular movement going through its various stages. If m is accumulated for use as capital we could think of extended reproduction as being represented by an outward spiral movement.

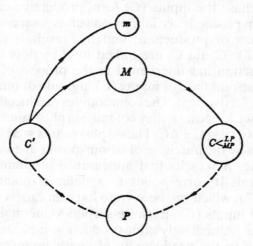

Figure 7.1 Circuit of capital

Industrial capital changes successively into its three forms: money capital (M), productive capital (P), and commodity capital (C'). Each form presupposes the existence of the other forms because it presupposes the circuit itself. This allows us to distinguish the function of each of the forms of capital from its function as capital. In societies where they exist, money, factor inputs and commodities can always function as means of payment, means of production, and a depository of exchange value respectively, but they only act as capital when they follow these functions in the circuit of capital. Then, money-capital acts as a means of purchasing labour-power, productive capital acts as a means of producing surplus value, and commodity-capital acts as the depository of surplus value.

In the movement through the circuit we can identify two spheres of activity: production and circulation. The sphere of production lies between C and C'. It was Marx's abstraction to define all value as being added in the sphere of production by living labour which also preserved the value of constant capital. This has profound implications for his theory of distribution because it explains what it is he is describing as being distributed. The sphere of circulation contains the process of exchange between C' and C. Even if capital and labour are used in the exchange process they add no value to output!

This assumption seems strange to orthodox economists because they are usually interested in obtaining a price theory by aggregating factors used in production and exchange. But Marx is interested in the social relations of distribution, and in particular the method of distributing value as he defines it, since this would reveal the likely role to be played by income recipients in class struggle. Thus, whilst commercial capital adds no value, this does not prevent its receiving a share of value according to the appropriate distributional relations which characterise capitalism (see Chapter 12).

When we have constructed the circuit of capital in circular form, we see that it becomes arbitrary to open and close the circuit with money capital, just as a circle has no beginning nor end. Note that the money circuit contains the interruption of the sphere of circulation by the sphere of production. In characterising capital as self-expanding value we found that the capitalist's motive was to buy in order to sell dearer. So, for capital seen from the perspective of the money circuit, production appears as a necessary but unfortunate interruption in the process of money-making. Merchants' capital can avoid this interruption, although it depends upon production elsewhere, but industrial capital cannot. If a nation's capital is seized by the attempt to make profit without the unavoidable link of production, it may find itself in a speculative boom which eventually crashes when the economy is brought back to the reality of the need for production.

Marx also analyses the circuit from two other perspectives, from productive capital and from commodity-capital. The circuit of productive capital begins and ends with P, production, and so the purpose of the circuit appears to be production, and, in so far as surplus value is accumulated, production on an extended scale. In contrast to the money circuit, for the productive circuit, the sphere of circulation appears as a necessary but unwanted intervention in the sphere of production . Economists more often than capitalists tend to ignore this necessary mediation by exchange, and we can cite neo-classical and von Neumann growth theory in this context. Nevertheless a capitalist who unwittingly or otherwise produces a growing inventory of commodities with the expectation or hope of sale is soon brought back to reality with the loss of working capital. It is not sufficient to produce (surplus) value, it has to be realised.

The circuit of commodity-capital begins and ends with C', and so the purpose of the circuit appears to be to generate consumption. As the sphere of circulation is followed by the sphere of production, neither sphere is interrupted by the other, so neither appears as evil or unnecessary. Capital, seen from this perspective, is reflected in neo-classical general equilibrium theory, where supply and demand harmoniously interact as production and exchange to yield final consumption. It leads to the popular myth that the purpose of production is consumption (and so not profit or exchange).

We have described the three circuits of capital which together form the circuit as a whole. One might wonder why there are not four circuits of capital, with each 'node' on the circuit (P, C', M and C) forming a starting and finishing point. The reason why $C <^{LP}_{MP}$ is not the basis for a circuit of capital is that the C is not capital. The means of production purchased in this C may be another capitalist's commodity production and hence commodity-capital. However, labour-power is never capital until it is purchased, and then it becomes productive capital and not commodity-capital, which must contain produced surplus value. Thus, whilst from a technical point of view capitalism can be self-reliant for raw materials, it depends upon the social reproduction of labour-power from outside the pure system of production. This entails the use of political, ideological and legal as well as economic power. The point is to get the labourer to work. The same problems do not exist in getting a machine to work.

As we have hinted above, views of capital's process of reproduction corresponding to each circuit of capital can be constructed. These need not be uncritical of capitalism, but individually they are always inadequate, stressing one or more of the processes of production, consumption, exchange, profit-making and accumulation at the expense of the others. Only fleetingly, as they enter the circuit, do labour-power and produced means of production appear separated and then, not forming capital, they do not generate a view of the circuit as a whole. As a result orthodox economic theories can eliminate class relations altogether. Where they do enter it is inevitably as distributional or exchange (for example, effective demand) relations, and not those of production.

The money circuit suggests models of exchange. For the economy the matching of supply and demand becomes the be all and end all. Capital and labour are merely seen as productive services, either in full employment or a Keynesian unemployment equilibrium. Difficulties are merely associated with the informational services performed by the price (and interest rate) mechanism. The productive circuit attempts to ignore the market. This yields an excellent input–output theory for a planned economy, but this bears faint resemblance to capitalism. The commodity circuit sees the harmonious interaction of the purpose, consumption, and of the means, production. It is the strength of Marx's circuit of capital to expose the limitations of these outlooks. At the same time it reveals the functions of the forms in which capital appears and constructs a basis on which major economic categories and phenomena can be understood.

8

Economic Reproduction

In the previous chapter, a single circuit of industrial capital was examined. For capital as a whole, there are a large number of different circuits, each moving at its own pace and each expanding at its own rate, and these circuits must be integrated with each other. Marx analyses these matters in Volume II of *Capital* by dividing the economy into two broad sectors, Department I involved in the production of means of production (i.e. constant capital, c) and Department II concerned with the production of means of consumption (purchased by workers out of variable capital, v, and by capitalists out of surplus value, s).

In Figure 8.1, balance between the two sectors is illustrated by use of a flow diagram. The two circuits for the two departments, $M_I - C_I \ldots P_I \ldots C'_I - M'_I$ and $M_{II} - C_{II} \ldots P_{II} \ldots C'_{II} - M'_{II}$ are shown (although M'_I and M'_{II} are absorbed into a central pool of money, M. In addition, there are commodity flows, with workers buying consumption goods from Department II with their wages v_I and v_{II}, and capitalists buying means of production, c_I and c_{II}, from Department I. Capitalists also buy consumption goods with surplus value, s_I and s_{II}.

If capitalists spend all of their surplus value on consumption, it is possible for the economy to reproduce itself at the same level of activity, what Marx called simple reproduction. But this implies a certain balance between the two

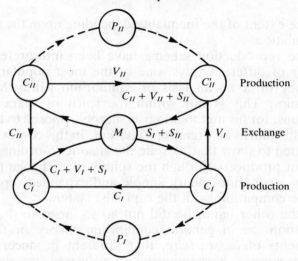

Figure 8.1 Economic reproduction

Departments. This can been seen in terms of equality between supply and demand for either of the two Departments. For Department I:

$$c_I + v_I + s_I = c_I + c_{II}$$

For Department II:

$$c_{II} + v_{II} + s_{II} = v_I + v_{II} + s_I + s_{II}$$

Each of these simplifies to give:

$$v_I + s_I = c_{II}$$

Once capital accumulation takes place, then capitalists' purchases must switch from Department II to Department I (to provide for more production of constant capital, although Department II production will be sustained to the extent that more money is advanced by capitalists to purchase more labour-power). It follows that for this expanded reproduction:

$$v_I + s_I > c_{II}$$

with the extent of the inequality depending upon the rate of accumulation.

These reproduction schema have been interpreted in a number of different ways, one of the most popular being that they offer an analysis of equilibrium within Marxist economics. This is not within the spirit of Marx's own intentions, for his methodology is sharply opposed to the use of equilibrium as an organising concept. In this context, he is concerned to show that, despite the chaotic co-ordination of different producers through the sphere of exchange (rather than by a conscious plan), simple and expanded reproduction are compatible with the capitalist system.

On the other hand, he did not go so far as to draw the implication, as in general equilibrium theory or for the proponents of *laissez-faire*, that different producers (and consumers) are harmoniously co-ordinated through the market at high levels of employment of resources. Rather Marx's schema points to two separate balances that have to be established.

The first is in values, as has already been illustrated. The second is in use-values. The appropriate quantities of commodities have to be produced and exchanged with each other. According to the schema above, the value quantities displayed have an unspecified quantitative relationship to the use values involved. This is clearly demonstrated by the hypothetical exercise of doubling the productivity (halving the values) of the commodities in one Department whilst leaving those in the other unchanged. As a result, the use-value balance will be disrupted (although the value balance remains the same), showing that the two balances are to a degree independent of each other. They are not entirely independent of each other in so far as such productivity change, for example, leads to the transfer of resources between the two Departments. This involves the co-ordination across the economy between the two balances already specified together with the complementary flows of money and the price system. Some of these issues are taken up in later chapters.

Meanwhile, the diagram of economic reproduction can be used to reinforce the (false or partial) views of the economy which were presented in the light of the single circuit of capital in the previous chapter. Little is added qualitatively, but the figure suggests what might be considered to be the factors determining the level of economic activity. Note first that economic theory and ideology tend to focus on the central 'box' of exchange activity, relative to which the two spheres of production appear to be extraneous. Generally, this supports the erroneous view that production can be taken for granted or that it is simply a technical relation that forms the unproblematic basis for exchange relations.

This is most apparent for neo-classical general equilibrium theory (or *laissez-faire* economics) where exchange relations are considered to be sufficient to guarantee equality of supply and demand at full employment of economic resources. And, in stability analysis, it becomes a question of whether disproportion between the various quantities embodied within the circuits are self-correcting through price movements in response to excess supplies and demands.

For Keynesian theory, the role of aggregate demand becomes determinant. If we focus on the investment multiplier then the level of $c_I + c_{II}$ assumes a central role. More generally, if we also include the role of consumption, then the expenditure on this out of national income, $v_I + v_{II} + s_I + s_{II}$ becomes important. In this form, the consumption function has more affinity with the Kalecki–Kaldor method of determining aggregate demand (where income is divided down into wages and profits). But the important point remains that the decisive influence on the level of aggregate economic activity is given by (a particular set of) expenditure flows within the economy with, in Marx's terms, no role for the production of surplus value and the conflict over this fundamental economic relation.

A more sophisticated Keynesian economics includes the role of money. In this respect, the level of economic activity is determined by the size of the flows of money that stream out of the central pool, M. Restrict these and the economy falters. According to the theory of liquidity preference, interest rates that are too high to generate full employment, but which are expected to rise, give rise to speculative holding of money at the expense of expenditure so that

aggregate demand is too low. The respective roles of the
banking system and the rate of interest are taken up later.
Here it is important to note that the source of unemployment is to be found in insufficient exchange activity, almost
irrespective of the ability of the economy to generate
profitability. In Keynes's own theory, this depended to a
large extent on waves of pessimism, in which poor expectations about business profitability (and high expectations
about interest rates) prove self-fulfilling prophecies. More
generally, and in significantly different ways, recent
developments within economic theory have given expectations a considerably enhanced role in determining the path
of the economy.

Finally, a more radical theory of the economy views the
level of economic activity to be determined by distributional
relations between capital and labour. Such a view is
associated ideologically with both the right and the left, with
the former arguing that the power of trade unions needs to
be curbed to restore profitability, and the latter that the
conflicts involved are irreconcilable within the confines of
capitalism.

Analytically, this outlook depends on a 'fixed cake'
understanding of the economy in which national income v_I
$+ v_{II} + s_I + s_{II}$ is divided between the two classes with one
gaining only at the expense of the other. If wages, as
represented by $v_I + v_{II}$, rise too much then profits, as
represented by $s_I + s_{II}$, must fall, and this undermines the
motive and the ability to accumulate.

This view of the economy, although usually included
within Marxist theory under the label of the Sraffian or
neo-Ricardian school (a critique of which is to be found in
Chapter 10), does diverge from Marx's own presentation of
the structure of the capitalist economy. For the central role
of distribution as decisive in determining profitability is only
possible by confining the analysis to (one part of) the arena
of exchange. Once the sphere of production is incorporated
as well, the apparent symmetry between capital and labour,
in distributional relations and in receiving profits and wages
out of national income, evaporates, for the payment of
wages is a precondition for the production process to begin

(or, more exactly, this is true of the purchase of labour-power, whose actual payment may well come later). Profits are the result or outcome of the production process rather than the shares of the spoils after wages have been paid. Consequently, distributional relations between capital and labour are not of the 'fixed cake' variety, even if, obviously, *ceteris paribus* profits are higher if wages are lower (although Keynesians might argue otherwise in view of inadequate demand). Rather, profits depend first and foremost on the ability of capitalists to extract surplus value from the production process; they need, whatever the level of wages, to coerce labour to work over and beyond the labour time required to produce those wages. Thus it might be concluded that for Marx the production of absolute and relative surplus value is crucial to the understanding of distributional relations, but that the latter cannot be read off from production conditions alone.

9

Crises

The nature of crises

Capitalism will be in or on the verge of a crisis whenever the social accumulation of capital is interrupted. In such a circumstance the working class will be posed with two alternatives. It may concede an economic, political or social defeat to restore capital to its normal condition of reproduction on an extended scale. This could, for example, involve a fall in wages or employment, the fighting of a war, or an upheaval in working conditions. Alternatively the working class can overthrow the system of capitalist production. Marx believed that crises were endemic to capitalism, and in this sense alone revolution against capitalism was inevitable. For, again and again, the working class would take defeat, but with the lesson of defeat and its growing strength and organisation, defeat would eventually be inflicted on the *bourgeoisie* at the hands of the proletariat.

Marx's theory of the inevitability of crises depends upon his law of the tendency of the rate of profit to fall. This law will be discussed in the next chapter. For the moment it should be observed that crises in capitalism can occur apart from movements in the rate of profit and indeed from outside the pure circuit of capital, with social upheaval not directly economic in character. However, for capitalism, in contrast to other modes of production, these extraneous

54

factors (such as war, natural disaster, or political instability) are rarely the causes of economic crises but are more likely to be consequences. This is because of capital's high development of the productive forces, which brings with it power over nature and economic control of civil society. On the other hand, this means that the cause of crises must be placed in the economic system and not in 'random' events.

Marx emphasises that crises could always arise because of the contradiction between the production of social use-values and their individual or, more exactly, private consumption. It is only under capitalism, where production for exchange rather than use dominates, that overproduction of a commodity can prove an embarrassment. Elsewhere it would be a cause for celebration, because it would mean increased consumption. But for capital, consumption is not enough, profit must be realised as well. This depends upon sale, and if this becomes impossible production may be curtailed and capital operate on a reduced scale. This applies to a single set of capitalists producing a particular commodity. They may have been subject to some disturbance generated within the economic sphere (see Chapter 5) or elsewhere. However, it must not be forgotten that the reproduction of their capitals on an extended scale is intimately integrated with other circuits of capital. Their demands for inputs may be another capitalist's supply and vice versa, and so on to other capitalists. The economy may be seen as a system of expanding circuits linked together like interlocking cog-wheels. If one set of wheels grinds to a halt or slows down, so may others throughout the system. For the clothing industry to be expanded there must first have been excess production of textiles, requiring a higher produce of flax and cotton and more machinery. On the other hand there must be (or be created) a demand for machinery already produced, raw materials and consumption goods. A single economic event, for example the demand for a shirt, works with a snowball effect. In this context Keynes introduced the term 'multiplier', which through aggregate demand has a multiplicative effect on income: an increase in production (by, say, 100) creates extra income, this in turn inducing new purchases. Eventually production and income will reach a level higher than the original change (for example, 400). It is the necessary but unplanned interlocking of capitals that leads Marx to talk of the anarchy of capitalist production.

What we have been examining is the breakdown of an individual capitalist's circuit of capital and the possible social consequences given private decisions on production and purchase. We pursue this further on the assumption that commodities exchange at their values. A circuit of capital may be broken in any of its links (see Figure 7.1). The break may be either voluntary or involuntary on the part of the capitalist, being unwilling but able or willing but unable to allow the circuit to continue. In the first case the capitalist will be speculating. Either it is anticipated that profitability may be increased by delaying the circuit, or it is hoped to create or exploit a monopoly position by doing so. In the second case the capitalist is subject to forces beyond immediate control.

There is unlikely to be a break of the circuit in the sphere of production provided labour does not take industrial action and there are no technical or natural disasters. Thus almost all crises will appear to originate in the sphere of circulation as an inability or unwillingness to buy or sell. Consider the arm $M-C <^{LP}_{MP}$. A voluntary break here implies that C could be bought, but the owner of the M presumably anticipates a lower price for the inputs or hopes to create such a lower price. In particular, for the labour input, this may be done by imposing a lock-out. On the other hand the break in the circuit could be involuntary. The owners of the inputs may attempt to create or exploit a monopoly position – in particular labour may strike. Alternatively inputs may not be available because, in the previous round of social production, outputs – partly present inputs – may have been produced in the wrong proportions. This will provide for an excess demand of a particular commodity and necessarily an excess supply in some other sector. If this situation becomes generalised across many producers we may describe the situation as a crisis of disproportionality. These remarks need to be modified if the commodity in short supply is labour-power. Then there will be an excess demand for labour but also an excess supply of unused money-capital.

A break in the sphere of circulation may also appear between C' and M. A capitalist may speculate about the future price of commodity-capital in case of a voluntary break. Alternatively it may be impossible to sell produce. This means the commodity is in excess supply. This could be because of a disproportionality (see previous paragraph), or alternatively those who normally buy the commodity may be unable to do so because they do not have money to hand. If other circuits have been broken, for whatever reason, workers, capitalists and others will not receive their regular flow of money income and hence will not make a regular flow of money expenditures. If this last situation becomes generalised we talk of a crisis of underconsumption.

Marxists have usually looked at crises of underconsumption and disproportionality by dividing the economy into two sectors, investment and consumption, following Marx's scheme for extended reproduction (as covered in Chapter 8). Some have argued that there is a persistent tendency for the supply of consumption goods to outstrip the demand for them, others that the tendency exists for a disproportionately large production of investment goods. Both are logically possible, but disproportions – overproduction in one sector, underproduction in another – are just as likely to occur within the consumption and investment goods sectors as between the two as aggregates. In all this it is possible to confuse a crisis of disproportionality, in which consumption goods are in excess supply, with a crisis of underconsumption. This last will be characterised by a general overproduction of commodities and excess capacity and must be generated by some 'exogenous' disturbance. A crisis of disproportionality does not presuppose such an 'exogenous' disturbance but may be one, tending to generate a crisis of underconsumption.

Breaks in individual circuits of capital will occur infinitely often given the anarchy of capitalist production, fluctuations in market prices, the vagaries of the credit system, speculation, monopolisation, and the economic obsolescence of fixed capital with technological progress. Occasionally a crisis will be generated, its extent depending upon the pattern of adjustment in disequilibrium. This is nothing

more or less than a Keynesian analysis of the multiplier,
yielding an unemployment equilibrium for underconsumption and a 'bottleneck' disequilibirum for disproportionality.
It describes and demonstrates the possibility of crises. Marx
put the whole matter rather neatly when he suggested that
commodities are in love with money but the course of true
love never did run smooth.

But this leaves aside the motive of capitalist production:
profit. The most important factor from the capitalist's
standpoint is the amount of profit thrown off by the circuit of
capital. All obstacles to the circuit's movement may be
overcome if m is large enough. Should profitability be
improving, capitalists will be reluctant to speculate, deny
wage increases, or in any way hinder the process of
money-making. Crises will not be generated. In the last
analysis a potential cause of a crisis is more than likely to be
insignificant, given sufficient profitability. Profits can pay
and pave the way.

However, should the ability to expand the production of
profit be constrained, then not only will some capitalists
be expelled from production by bankruptcy, but general
pessimism will reign, production will be curtailed, and a
crisis will be generated. Movements in profitability depend
upon movements in values. But, as we have seen, the
process of competitive accumulation brings frequent reduc-
tions in the values of all commodities. It is a contradictory
feature of capital that individual profit is pursued by
reducing values through relative expulsion of living labour,
which is the source of surplus value, from production. Thus
accumulation in pursuit of profitability may prove unsuccess-
ful. Marx analyses this in the context of the law of the
tendency of the rate of profit to fall.

On the Falling Rate of Profit

Marx's theory of the law of the tendency of the rate of profit to fall (LTRPF) has been extremely controversial, in terms of its validity, its interpretation and its significance. In this chapter the attempt will be made to outline Marx's law and to answer some of the criticisms that have been levelled against it. In much of the literature, Marx's analysis has been treated too simplistically, as a set of algebraic propositions that have been asserted to be correct, incorrect or somewhere in between. On the other hand, Marx's contribution has often been removed to the realm of high philosophy, in which the law takes on the character of an abstract truth, something derived from the logic of capital itself.

The position adopted here differs from both of these, admittedly parodied, extremes. However, the argument is a complex one, depending upon conceptual rather than algebraic argument. As a result, the structure of the analysis is summarised first and is followed by a more detailed account containing elaboration and justification.

Summary of the argument

1. Marx's LTRPF is based upon a fundamental conceptual

distinction between the organic composition of capital (OCC) and the value composition of capital (VCC).

2. The OCC measures the results of accumulation by exclusive reference to the sphere of production, i.e. surplus value creation, whilst the VCC reflects this process in the sphere of exchange, i.e. (surplus) value realisation or formation, which should not be understood simply as or confined to the problem of sale.

3. The rise of the OCC associated with the specifically capitalist methods of production is the source of the law as such, whilst the formation of the VCC is associated with the counteracting tendencies (CTs). These two tendencies are essential and underlying aspects of the accumulation process which interact to form more complex economic phenomena, but only for that stage of development of capitalism for which machine production is predominant.

4. This implies that the LTRPF (and the CTs) is an abstract law in that it does not give immediate predictions about movements in the rate of profit. In other words, it is not an empirical law in this narrowly predictive sense, but it does provide the basis on which more complex and immediate economic phenomena can be studied by the inclusion of further historical and logical analysis.

5. The presentation of Marx's LTRPF in this way leads to a complete contrast with the understanding and criticism of it associated with Okishio and which has been taken up by the Sraffian school of economics. Because this latter analysis employs comparative statics, which is based on equilibrium analysis, it treats the accumulation process as one which engenders a harmonious interaction between production and circulation. Consequently, the theory can be characterised as the dialectical opposite of Marx's.

The compositions of capital

In Volume I of *Capital*, Marx examines the specifically capitalist method of production, i.e. the systematic way in which capitalism seizes and transforms the labour process.

The resulting rise in the technical composition of capital, TCC, that accompanies accumulation can be measured by a single index only in so far as a mass of heterogeneous raw materials (and living labour) is reduced to a common denominator. For orthodox theory, this is an index number problem. In Marx's theory, the values of commodities are the basis on which the TCC can be measured. This is not simply the choice of one index rather than another. It reflects Marx's previously developed proposition in the opening chapters of *Capital* that value, understood as socially necessary labour time, is a legitimate category of analysis for a commodity-producing society, since such a society brings different concrete labours into equivalence with each other, thereby creating value relations within that society as a social relation. Consequently, it is legitimate to measure the TCC in value terms, not for convenience with the drawbacks associated with any index number, but as the expression of the changing conditions of production in terms of the social (and value) relations in which they are embodied. In other words, the measurement of the TCC by values is not a more or less convenient and arbitrary index of changing production conditions, but a conceptualisation of part of the accumulation process.

These comments are borne out when the ways of constructing the value measure of the TCC are analysed. Marx distinguishes between the value and organic compositions. In the literature these have rarely been distinguished, and the two have been used interchangeably, usually according to the terminology adopted by Marx for the subject under consideration. For both, the algebraic definition has been denoted by C/V, but this begs the question of what values are used to reduce the heterogeneous bundle of raw materials – in the case of C – and of living labour – in the case of V – to a single value dimension. This is a pertinent problem in this context, since the whole analysis is concerned with accumulation, in which the production of relative surplus value is motivated by the wish to reduce, i.e. to change, the values of commodities.

Before dealing with this problem in the 'dynamic' context of accumulation, it is useful for expositional purposes to distinguish the VCC and the OCC in a 'static' context. Consider, for example, the production of jewellery. Let us suppose that exactly the same labour process is used to produce both silver and gold rings. Both production processes will have the same TCC, since this measures the mass of raw materials to living labour. But the production of gold rings will involve a higher VCC since it uses raw materials of a higher value. To reflect the lack of difference in the production processes from the technical point of view, Marx defined the OCC as equal for the two sectors. It is supposed to measure the TCC in value terms, leaving aside the differences created by the greater or lesser value of the raw materials employed.

This creates some difficulty in measuring the OCC, since the appropriate values at which to define the ratio of C to V are not specified. Should we, for example, use the value of gold, the value of silver or something in between for the definition? This is a problem created by the attempt to make the distinction in a static context. It is only when production processes are changing that the distinction between the OCC and the VCC has any significance, for otherwise the TCC alone is adequate to specify the equivalence or otherwise between production processes from the organic point of view.

Let us consider another example. Suppose that there is a reduction in the value of steel, but otherwise nothing else changes. Then the VCC in any one sector will change accordingly to the relative content of steel in the production of its constant capital and in the value of labour-power. Given an equal composition of the various skills of labour between sectors, then the VCCs will vary according to their relative use of steel. Nevertheless, the OCCs across the sectors have remained unchanged, because there has been no change in the TCCs. The OCC simply measures changes in production in value terms and so is only of interest, as distinct from the VCC, when the TCC is changing. Then it can measure something distinct from the VCC, which measures changes in the TCC only after account has been taken of the changing values of commodities, as they are realised in exchange. The two examples given above only serve to explain the difference between the VCC and the OCC. They do not have much significance in themselves.

The matter is different once we begin to consider changing conditions of production. Marx argues that, at its developed stage, capitalism involves accumulation through the production of relative surplus value with the use of machinery to displace living labour. This results in a rising TCC which can be measured in value terms by the OCC from the point of view of changes in production alone. Raw materials and labour power enter the production process with definite values, and this leads to a definite ratio of constant to variable capital, according to the extent that labour is coerced to transform inputs into outputs. If we were to put it chronologically, the OCC measures the TCC at the 'old' values prevailing prior to the renewal of the production process.

This results, however, in a change (reduction) in the values of commodities. When these enter the market, correspondingly new values are established in the form of market values. The VCC is measured at this stage. Necessarily, it takes account of the TCC from the point of view of the change both in the OCC and in the values of commodities as they are realised in the sphere of exchange. To put it chronologically, the VCC is measured at the 'new' rather than at the 'old' values.

The description of the difference between the VCC and the OCC in terms of new and old values is slightly misleading, since the distinction is conceptual rather than chronological. At any moment in time, some capitals will be entering the production process as others will be leaving it. What the distinction does is to draw upon and build a separation between the spheres of production and exchange. In production, the two classes of capital and labour confront each other over the process of production and, as accumulation proceeds, there is a tendency for the OCC to rise. In exchange, capitalists confront each other as competitors in the process of buying and selling and, as accumulation proceeds, there is a tendency for values to be reduced and for the VCC to rise less than the OCC. It is the interaction of these processes, as understood in the structural separation between production and exchange, that is the concern of Marx's LTRPF.

The law as such and the counteracting tendencies

Marx's treatment of the LTRPF occupies three chapters in Volume III of *Capital*. The first is entitled 'The Law as Such'. It contains what appears to be a simple algebraic derivation of falling profitability. Since the rate of profit may, in value terms, be written as $r = e/(OCC+1)$, where e is the rate of surplus value, a fall in r is immediate from the previously derived rising OCC, provided there is no rise in e. From our previous discussion, it should be clear that this law cannot be interpreted as a prediction about empirical movements in the rate of profit, since discussion of the OCC is restricted to changes in the production process without any reference to changes in the values of commodities. This explains why the constant value of e is not so much an assumption as an expression of the unchanging values of commodities during production, so that there is no reduction in the value of labour power.

Marx's second chapter deals with the CTs. These fall into two types. There are those that follow from the changes in values, resulting from the rising OCC. If we write $r = S/(C+V)$, it follows that anything that reduces C or V and anything that increases S tends to increase r. The production of relative surplus value tends to do all of these by increasing productivity and reducing the value of C, V (whether directly in the wage goods sector or indirectly through its use of lower valued raw materials) and increasing S through the reduction of V. These changes in the values of commodities are synonymous with the formation of the VCC.

In addition, Marx considers CTs of a less systematic variety, which do not follow directly and of necessity from accumulation, such as the paying of lower wages to those pulled into backward conditions of employment from the reserve army of labour, the cheapening of raw materials and wage goods through foreign trade, and the formation of joint stock companies which, by virtue of their large mass of less risky capital, yield a lower rate of return than the general rate of profit. This group of CTs does not follow of necessity from the rising OCC, even though they can be seen to be necessary, if contingent, results of capitalist development. Marx appears to lump them together with the others without separating them analytically. This may be explained by the lack of final preparation of Volume III for publication. In addition, Marx's list of CTs follows closely that of J. S. Mill, suggesting that he had yet to rework his material properly. Mill's treatment of the law follows that of Ricardo and is based upon the declining productivity of agriculture, rather than, as with Marx, the increasing productivity of all sectors.

It is this treatment of the CTs by Marx which makes it appear as though he is dealing with immediate movements in *r* as a numerical counterweight to the law as such. Certainly, the CTs are presented at a more complex level of analysis than the law, for, as we have seen, they involve the formation of the VCC which incorporates changes both in production and exchange. However, like the law, the CTs should not be seen as factors of empirical weight directly governing movements in the rate of profit, but as embodying those processes that transform the changing conditions of production into movements in exchange.

The internal contradictions of the law

In the previous section we have interpreted both the law and the CTs as being directed at capturing abstract, underlying processes rather than as predicting immediate movements in the rate of profit. This follows from a more general interpretation of a law or tendency in this way. For example, when it is argued that there is a *tendency* for rates of profit to be equalised across sectors as a result of capital mobility, this should be seen, not as a prediction of equal rates of profit, but as one process among others governing capital accumulation. It is only in orthodox economics that this tendency is seen as an actuality, so that an equilibrium can be constructed in which all profit rates are equalised. In contrast, for Marx, laws and tendencies have to be located in the context of the more complex form in which they manifest themselves. In this case, the tendency for the rate of profit to be equalised has to be set against the competition between capitalists to differentiate their rates of profit from the average, whether this be through accumulation to increase productivity, the paying of lower wages, or whatever.

This is the basis on which we should examine Marx's third chapter on the LTRPF, aptly named 'The Internal Contradictions of the Law'. He examines the law and the CTs as a contradictory unity of underlying tendencies which gives rise to more complex empirical phenomena. Consequently, the analysis is more concerned with the antagonistic coexistence of the law and its CTs than with the prediction of movements in the rate of profit. The two tendencies cannot be added together algebraically to give a rise or fall in the rate of profit according to which of the two is the stronger. Rather, it is concerned with the contradictions between the production of circulation of (surplus) value as the process of value-creation and formation proceeds on the basis of existing values, even as these are reduced by the accumulation of capital.

That the LTRPF concerns the interaction of abstract tendencies is implicitly confirmed by Marx's analysis of the internal contradictions. There is little or no discussion of movements in the rate of profit, and a much greater concern with the ability of the economy to be able to accumulate the mass of surplus value that it has been able to produce. There is a greater focus on whether accumulation can be sustained than on whether it generates a higher or lower rate of profit.

In this light, the CTs can be reinterpreted. If the reduction in the values of constant and variable capital have been realised, then this is indicative of the translation of changes in conditions of production into the sphere of exchange. On the other hand, the formation of joint stock companies, the exploitation of the reserve army of labour and the opening up of foreign trade become conditions conducive to a continuing accumulation irrespective of the rate of profit at which they occur.

Nor is the consideration of the LTRPF as an abstract law

to deny it of any empirical significance. Marx's main conclusion is that the law and CTs cannot exist side by side in harmony, but must at times give rise to crises. This requires careful interpretation, for there is certainly no axiomatic derivation of the necessity of crises, just as there is no axiomatic derivation of a falling rate of profit. Rather Marx is pointing to the *immanent* possibility of crises, just as he had previously done so in Volume II of *Capital* as a result of the more narrow potential of disjuncture between sale and purchase on the basis of unchanging values. For the LTRPF, however, a source of disjuncture is identified in the accommodation in exchange of changing values from production.

This leads to further empirical implications of the LTRPF, for it suggests that crises which owe their origins to developments in the sphere of production will, nevertheless, break in the sphere of circulation. This is one reason why the LTRPF is liable to lead empirically to actual falls in the rate of profit. As the accumulation process falters, the mass of profit realised tends to be set against an unchanging mass of fixed capital, so that profitability declines. But this need not be so. If, for example, as a result of bankruptcies, large masses of capital are depreciated or bought up by surviving capitalists at rock bottom prices, then the rate of profit may even rise as a result of the ensuing crisis.

This point illustrates that the falling rate of profit has been something of a fetish in the literature, whatever the position adopted in relation to Marx's own analysis. The focus has been on whether theory can produce a fall in the rate of profit or not, by whatever mechanism, whether it be a rising OCC or by a rise in wages at the expense of profits. Once the rate of profit falls, it is presumed that the economy collapses into crisis as a result of deficient investment on the part of capitalists, this in turn leading to deficient demand for potential output as in Keynesian theory. In this perspective there is a complete separation between the theory that yields the fall in profitability and the theory of the results of that fall, i.e. between the cause and the course of the crisis.

However, it cannot even be presumed that a fall in profitability results in a crisis. There may be a reduced incentive and capacity to accumulate in terms of reward, but some reward is better than none. Continuing accumulation may be necessary to preserve existing (fixed) capital and, most important of all, falling profitability acts as a coercive competitive force. Consequently, as capitalists attempt to restore profitability, they may accumulate at a faster rate than previously!

For Marx, the generation of crises through proximate falls in the rate of profit is a possibility, but this does not offer a penetrating analysis of the cause and course of crises. If the LTRPF is understood as the combination of contradictory tendencies uniting production and exchange, then the examination of these tendencies, at the more complex level of their interaction, opens the way to an analysis of crises linked to and based upon the accumulation process.

At the general level, this requires an analysis of value production and formation in exchange in a much wider context than is presented in the opening chapters of *Capital*. There, the category of value is understood as a social relation which establishes an equivalence between different types of concrete labour, thereby creating the category of abstract labour. There will be different skills of labour as well as different types of labour. Within each sector, there can be different levels of productivity. But commodity equivalence through exchange is a melting pot that reduces all of these labours to the common denominator of value. With accumulation and the competition to reduce values, socially necessary labour time (SNLT) in each sector becomes the centre around which individual values in the sector revolve.

This creates a new task for value, and it is one which is intimately related to the LTRPF. Since accumulation leads to a reduction in SNLT, the whole concept of value appears to be at risk, for we are attempting to utilise a category whose quantification through labour time of production is upset as soon as it is established. This is not so, however, once we recognise that the equivalence established between different types of labour is extended through time to labours of different productivity. The OCC, for example, is constructed on the basis of equivalence for previously established values, whereas the formation of the VCC is the process of establishing those values in the wake of the changing production conditions associated with the rising OCC.

We can go no further than this without specifying the nature of the interaction between the law and the CTs. This can be done by extending the logical analysis of the mechanisms by which value relations are expressed in exchange or by specifying particular historically developed conditions in which accumulation takes place. Here two examples of the former type of analysis are briefly embarked upon.

Fixed capital

It is apposite to study fixed capital in this context since, by definition, it passes value on to commodities over a time which exceeds the production period. It is during this time that there is a reduction both in the replacement value of this portion of constant capital, as productivity rises in the sector producing fixed capital, and in the value passed on to commodities by the fixed capital, as productivity rises in the sector where it is in operation. Let us consider the implications of this in terms of the lifetime of the fixed capital.

The value passed on by machinery to the raw materials that are worked up into commodities is only partly determined by the physical condition of the machinery. It is also dependent upon the formation of SNLT, which is determined in the sector as a whole and is, to a large extent, independent of production by any single capital. From this point of view the longer the machinery lasts, the more value it has preserved over its lifetime. There is a pressure to prolong the life of machinery for this reason, although the overall value produced cannot be increased by this means. If there is an increase in machine durability, for whatever reason, this results in a reduction in SNLT, as the constant capital preserved by depreciation of fixed capital is spread over a larger mass of commodities.

The previous paragraph analyses the turnover of fixed capital from the point of view of its use value in value production. We now look at the value of fixed capital from

the point of view of its own production. With the accumulation of capital, there tends to be a reduction in the value of
the machine, due to productivity increases in the sector
producing it as well as through productivity increases in the
raw materials with which it is made. In addition, there are
liable to be improvements in the quality of machinery. As a
result, from the point of view of the exchange value passed
on in the circulation process, the lifetime of the machinery
should be reduced to a minimum. This is so that its value can
be preserved in the commodities produced before it is incap-
able of adding positively to SNLT.

If we put these two factors together, we find that there are
pressures both to increase and to reduce the durability of
fixed capital. The formation of turnover time in practice will
reflect the equivalence created between the values of old,
continuing fixed capital and the new fixed capital. For
orthodox theory this conflict is resolved harmoniously within
vintage models by the smooth renewal of fixed capital
through the market mechanism. For Marxist theory there
can be violent movements in the value relations connecting
old and new fixed capital, so that the renewal of fixed capital
tends to follow a self-reproducing cycle.

The value of money

The second example of further logical development of the
LTRPF is to be found in the analysis of the value of money.
In the early chapters of Volume I of *Capital*, Marx
demonstrates how money acts as the social means of
measuring value in its property of general equivalent. As
already observed, once accumulation is proceeding, the
measure of value now has to perform the task of establishing
an equivalence between 'old' and 'new' values. Whether it
does so on the basis of a formal convertibility with a (gold)
commodity money or not, we will show that there are
competing pressures on changes in the value of money.
Since $1 + r = (C + V + S)/(C + V)$, it follows that profitability is
increased the greater output is relative to capital advanced.
However, in monetary terms, output is evaluated at prices
formed at a different time to those for inputs; this is

necessarily so, except by way of accident, since there has been an intervening change in values because of changing conditions of production. From the point of view of production of other commodities, there is pressure for the value of money to remain the same, so that the value of advanced capital is preserved in output, i.e. the value of output or new values is assessed on the market-place at the same values as the value of inputs or old values. From the point of view of circulation, however, and for the renewal of accumulation, there is pressure for the value of money to increase so that the value of capital advanced is reduced, this reflecting the reduced values that have been achieved in the previous period of production. This corresponds to the new values asserting themselves as SNLT at the expense of the old values.

Once again, it is the interaction of these two competing factors which establishes an equivalence between old and new values. In the previous example it did so through the formation of the turnover time of fixed capital. In this case it is the value of money that must emerge. According to orthodox theory, this can be done by the market mechanism with the two factors cancelling each other out to yield an equilibrium level of prices corresponding to full employment (or below full employment for Keynesian theory). For Marxist theory there can be no such presumption, and the value of money is subject to sharp fluctuations which correspond to and intensify crises of production. This is quite independent of whether the conditions of production of gold are relevant in establishing a value for this commodity which does itself diverge from the value that money represents in the process of exchange.

Although Marx laid the theoretical foundations for examining fixed capital in Volume II of *Capital*, he did not take his analysis much further. It is far from clear how this can be done, other than by an empirical study of the differing conditions of production. This lack of analysis is not reproduced in the case of the formation of the value of money. In his study of banking capital in Volume III, Marx provides a sophisticated extension of his theory of money by a logical analysis of the forms of capital in exchange and by a

corresponding empirical analysis of the British banking
system. Some of the theoretical content of this analysis is
presented in Chapter 12.

A response to Okishio

The major criticism of Marx's theory of the LTRPF has
evolved in recent years as a result of a theorem proved by
Okishio. Informally, he argued that the rate of profit cannot
fall unless real wages rise, given a wider availability of
techniques of production. In other words, a falling rate of
profit is contingent upon rising wages. In Okishio's interpretation of Marx, new techniques of production become
available to capitalists who adopt them if they are more
profitable than existing techniques at prevailing prices of
production. Once these new techniques are generalised
across the sectors concerned, this will result in a new set of
prices of production and a new rate of profit, equalised
across sectors. It is not only in the sectors where there has
been innovation that prices will change, because their,
presumably lower, prices will be passed on to the sectors in
which those commodities are used as inputs or as part of the
wage. Okishio asks whether the capitalists, acting blindly to
increase individual profitability by introducing new techniques, can paradoxically lead the system to a lower rate of
profit. Not surprisingly he comes up with a negative answer,
unless real wages are increased, and concludes that Marx is
incorrect. To put his result formally, suppose production
conditions are initially denoted by A and these are improved
to B. Let initial prices be a vector p and new prices be q,
initial rate of profit r and new rate of profit s. Then for a
given real bundle of wage goods w, s is greater than r.

It is important to recognise that Okishio's theorem, whatever its merits in interpreting (and refuting) Marx, is an
exercise in comparative statics, i.e. that it compares one
position of economic equilibrium with another. These
equilibria are constructed on the basis of a linear input-
output technology, denoted by the matrices A and B. This
use of comparative statics is already a peculiarity in the

context of the subject of enquiry, for if we are concerned with movements in the rate of profit as a source of crises, then it is inappropriate to adopt an equilibrium approach. If we move from one equilibrium to another, we cannot be analysing crises whatever happens to the rate of profit. There is one exception, and this is if the movements in the rate of profit are considered independently of, but as the source of, subsequent crises. We discussed this approach in the previous section. Here it comes up with the result that, first, we move from one equilibrium to another. Second, if the rate of profit falls, we have a crisis. Otherwise we do not. It is not clear, however, why the equilibrium, even with a lower rate of profit, would suddenly collapse into crisis.

This raises the much more interesting question of the movement between the two equilibria, rather than their comparison. This has not been analysed very much in the wake of the Okishio theorem, but it is motivated by the description of the way in which new techniques are introduced. By examining this process, it is apparent that, far from interpreting Marx's LTRPF, the approach associated with Okishio is its dialectical opposite! This is one reason why Marx may have blessed his analysis with the name of a law, since he saw the function of science as penetrating beneath the surface of appearances, in this case as they occur in the minds of individual capitalists and, presumably, academic economists such as the followers of Okishio.

Initially, an individual capitalist adopts a more advantageous technique of production, whether this be obtained through superior access to finance or technology. At initial prices p, this capitalist makes a higher rate of profit than the average level. Let this be denoted by $t > r$. From the perspective of the *individual* capitalist, the introduction of a new technique is associated with an increase in the rate of profit. This contrasts with Marx's analysis of the rising OCC, which leads to a tendency for falling profitability for *social* capital, since the evaluation of inputs and outputs at old values will lead to declining profitability.

Now we consider the generalisation of the new technique to all capitalists in the sector and the formation of new equilibrium prices and profit rate. It can be shown by techniques similar to those employed by Okishio that $t >$ $s > r$. In other words, the capitalist who had an original advantage finds that it is eroded as the source of the advantage is generalised across all other capitalists. The process of reducing prices, as a result of the introduction of the new technique, is one of reducing the rate of profit for the individual capitalist that had the initial advantage. Price formation out of technical change acts for the *individual* innovating capitalist as a pressure reducing the rate of profit. In contrast, for Marx, the process of price (VCC) formation out of technical change is a counteracting tendency to falling profitability for *social* capital, since it leads to a reduction in the value of constant and variable capital.

Now put the two processes, of introducing new technology and of generalising it to form new prices, together. Throughout, the processes for Okishio are immediate empirical phenomena. They interact to form algebraically a simple sum of effects that leads overall to a rise in profitability for the economy as a whole. Moreover, the two disequilibrium processes combine to cancel each other out and leave the system in harmonious equilibrium. Because of this, in the context of comparative statics, those who follow the Okishio approach never distinguish between the VCC and the OCC. Instead they rely exclusively upon an equilibrium notion of the VCC which, nevertheless, is given the name organic composition. By contrast, for Marx, the law and the CTs are underlying, abstract tendencies whose interaction is not some simple algebraic sum but a crisis-ridden path of accumulation.

Nevertheless, Okishio's result is a powerful one, since empirically the rate of profit can only fall if wages rise. This is allowed for in Marx's law, for, at old values, the value of labour power will represent an increasing bundle of wage goods as a result of productivity increase. This could precipitate a crisis, but in general accumulation prospers with rising real wages, as measured by the level of consumption as opposed to the value of labour-power. If real wages remain the same, then there is a reduction in the value of labour-power and an increase in the rate of surplus value. These are CTs for Marx. That they exist, as a result of accumulation, does not guarantee the absence of crisis.

11

The Transformation Problem

In Volume I of *Capital*, Marx is concerned with the production of value and surplus value, in Volume II with its exchange. A major part of Volume III deals with distributional relations as they arise out of the interaction of production with exchange.

For the distribution of surplus value between capitalists, Marx concentrates on the tendency for the rate of profit to be equalised across sectors of the economy. Forming a general rate of profit by $r = S/(C + V)$ where the value quantities S, C and V are aggregates for the economy as a whole, Marx argued that each capitalist would share in surplus value according to the share in capital advanced. It is as if each capitalist receives a dividend on an equity share in the economy as a whole. As a result, profit share would be $r(c_i + v_i)$ for the ith capitalist.

Corresponding to this would be a *price of production* for the commodity concerned, formed out of cost plus profit:

$$c_i + v_i + r(c_i + v_i)$$

A simple example will illustrate. Suppose there are just two capitalists, one of whom uses $60c + 40v$ and the other $40c +$

75

$60v$, with the rate of surplus value being 100 per cent. Then value for the first sector will be $60c + 40v + 40s$ and will be $40c + 60v + 60s$ for the second sector, with total values of 140 and 160 respectively. The general rate of profit is equal to 100/200 or 50 per cent. Since each capitalist shares equally in capital advanced (100), each must share equally in profit distributed (50 each). This can only come about if prices of production are each 150. This is despite the differences in the values between the two sectors.

Marx draws the conclusion that commodities do not exchange at their values but at prices of production which differ from values, as the composition of capital, c/v, is greater or less than the average for the economy as a whole. (Note that for the first, capital above $c/v = 2/3$ and for the second $c/v = 3/2$, compared with an average of 1 for the economy as a whole).

This apparent solution to the problem of the relationship between values and prices has perhaps been the most controversial aspect of Marxist economics. It has led some, even those sympathetic to Marxism, to reject the labour theory of value as irrelevant or even erroneous.

The reason for this is that Marx's solution to the transformation problem is perceived to be incorrect. He has shown that commodities no longer exchange at prices equal to their values but, in doing so, he has continued to evaluate inputs, c and v, (and the rate of profit) as if they were calculated at values. For the problem of translating given values into prices of production, this is indeed a serious deficiency, but one of which Marx was aware and which can easily be corrected. It is simply a matter of transforming the inputs as well as the outputs.

This has been done by a number of authors, although the algebra involved is not reproduced here. More significant is the observation that Marx's labour theory of value cannot founder on such quantitive conundrums, as the corrected algebraic solution indicates. He has shown, on the basis of the exchange system, that values exist as a consequence of the social relations between producers, so that price formation is a translation of production into exchange relations. As a result, values cannot be accepted or rejected according to whether algebraic solutions are considered satisfactory or not. Rather the relationship between values and prices has to be explored and established.

In this light, it is significant to note that the transformation problem as traditionally conceived focuses on the implications of differences in the value compositions of capital across different sectors in the economy. As it were, if a given amount of living labour in one sector (as employed through advance of variable capital v) works up more raw materials or more valuable raw materials (as represented by c) than in another sector, the commodities produced will command a higher price relative to value, as previously discussed and numerically illustrated.

But, in Volume III, Marx discusses the transformation problem entirely in terms of the organic composition of capital which, as has already been suggested in the chapter on falling profitability, is only concerned with the effects of the differing rates at which raw materials are transformed into outputs (rather than with the differing values of the inputs themselves). As such, Marx would appear to be justified in presuming that commodities as inputs enter the transformation problem as quantities of value (usually expressed by him in money terms). He is less concerned with how such inputs have previously obtained their values and prices, and more concerned with how differing organic compositions affect the process of price and profit formation.

This illustrates that Marx is dealing, not with equilibrium price theory as centred upon by orthodox theory (and orthodox interpretations of the transformation problem), but with the dynamic relation between changes in production and price formation. This acts in Volume III as a prelude to the treatment of the law of the tendency of the rate of profit to fall (although the order of presentation is reversed in this book). Generally, the transformation problem and the LTRPF have been considered as two separate problems (although an author's stance on each has often been read as a commitment for or against Marx's value theory). Here, through the consistent use of the OCC as distinguished from the VCC, it has been found that the two problems are

closely related to each other, since both are concerned with
the consequences of changes in conditions of production for
the tensions created by the integration of production with
exchange.

12

Banking Capital and the Theory of Interest

The purpose of this chapter is to outline Marx's theory of capital within the sphere of exchange. In earlier chapters the focus has primarily been on the role of capital in producing surplus value, with exchange as a necessary but unexplored accompaniment. But profits, and interest, are also to be found in capitalist activity other than in production. How are they to be examined relative to the earlier analysis?

Money and merchant's capital

One of the themes running through Marx's treatment of capital in exchange is that there is a crucial distinction to be made between money as money and money as capital. Money functions as money when it acts simply as a means of exchange between two agents, hence mediating commodity exchange, irrespective of the position of those agents in the circulation of capital as a whole – whether they be capitalists engaging in production or capitalists and workers engaging in consumption. In other words, the role of money as money is understood by reference to the formula for simple commodity circulation, $C-M-C$. By contrast, money as capital is understood by reference to the individual circuit of capital, $M-C \ldots P \ldots C'-M'$, where money is employed for the specific purpose of producing surplus value. Now, there is a definite relation between the two functions, since the exchanges of simple commodity circulation and of industrial production are ultimately connected, most notably when we recognise that $C-M$ for one agent is $M-C$ for another. Further, both the use of money as money and as capital can involve credit relations as money is lent and borrowed to perform the acts of exchange involved.

For Marx, however, the operation of money as money is seen as part of merchant's capital. Accordingly, it is necessary to begin with some comments on merchant's capital.

Marx makes clear at the outset that his treatment of merchant's capital is an abstract one. In practice, the functions of trading and producing (particularly the ambiguous role played by costs of circulation and distribution in functions such as transport) are to some extent intermingled. There is, however, a tendency for a separation between the two functions, and it must be reproduced in theory in order to comprehend the specific nature of merchant's capital which is the carrying out of exchange alone.

Apart from the division between industrial capital (which produces surplus value) and merchant's capital (which circulates it), an abstraction is involved in the division of merchant's capital itself into its two forms of commercial (buying and selling of commodities) and money-dealing capital, MDC (the handling of money).

With the development of capitalist production, merchant's capital and its two components become the specialised tasks of particular capitalists, thereby creating a division of 'labour' among them. Certain functions which arise from the commodity form of production become the specialised activity of money dealers. These include bookkeeping, the calculation and safeguarding of a money reserve, and the role of cashier. Now what is crucial for Marx's theory of merchant's capital, and consequently for MDC, is that it is subject to mobility with industrial capital and consequently exhibits a tendency to earn an average rate of profit even though it is not itself the source of surplus value (which can only be created by productive labour engaged by industrial capital).

Modified prices of production

A necessary implication is that the rate of return to MDC tends to be equalised to the rate of profit on industrial capital. More generally, the intervention of merchant's capital modifies the formation of prices of production, since capital advanced in the buying and selling of commodities shares in the surplus value distributed as profits. The addition of merchant costs (and profits on them) to price conforms to the sale of commodities at values, even if it appears as if commercial costs and profits are an addition to value. In other words, merchant costs and profits are made up by merchants buying at below value and selling at value.

Suppose, initially, that merchants simply use money of an amount B to perform their functions. Using the usual notation, it follows that capital advanced is now $C + V + B$. The rate of profit r equals $S/(C + V + B)$. Industrialists sell commodities at an aggregate price $(C + V)(1 + r)$ to merchants. These in turn add their profits to form selling price $(C + V)(1 + r) + Br = C + V + (C + V + B)r$. But $(C + V + B)r = S$, so that it follows that total selling price equals $C + V + S$, which is total value produced.

The situation is more complex when the merchants have costs other than the simple advance of money. These costs include means of production used in the process of circulation and variable capital advanced as commercial wages. Let these costs be K. Following the procedure used above, industrialists sell at $(C + V)(1 + r)$ and merchants sell at $(C + V)(1 + r) + Br + K(1 + r)$ in order to earn profit on money advances B as before and to recuperate costs K together with profit on them. For total selling price to remain equal to total value, it follows that $(C + V)(1 + r) + Br + K(1 + r) = C + V + S$. This yields $r = (S - K)/(C + V + B + K)$. Not surprisingly, the additional capital advances K are reflected in the denominator but, as costs, they are a deduction in the numerator from surplus value in the formation of the rate of profit.

Merchant's capital at a more complex level

A number of different aspects of merchant's capital have been analysed in their pure form, as the reflection of tendencies within the capitalist economy. At a more complex level there is a combination of these different elements. Merchant's capital is necessarily integrated with productive activity such as transport and storage, although this does not render all transport, etc. productive since some may derive from the functions of buying and selling. This appears to be problematic, since it would seem to be impossible to distinguish what is and what is not commercial activity. After all, the same lorry and driver may at the same time be undertaking both speculative and distributive activity on behalf of capital.

This problem is not subject to solution at the level of analysis at which it is posed; this, however, does not render redundant the distinction between merchant's and industrial capital. Just as merchant's capital is subject to a tendency to be confined to exchange activity, so it is never purely imprisoned there. It is most easily combined with other activities that are in principle organised as capitalist production, and transport and communication are the most obvious of candidates. Which these are is a matter of historical development. In the sweep of history, it is possible to point to the diminishing role covered by the activities of merchant's capital as it becomes subordinated to industrial capital. But this is by no means a linear progression, particularly in modern times, partly because of conglomeration and partly because of the rapid technical change that can take place in communications with the possibility of the commercial sector as its source or as its base.

What has just been argued applies equally to money-dealing capital as a part of merchant's capital. It is analysed in its pure form but cannot always be found like this. It is found incorporated both with industrial capital and with merchant's capital more generally. For an understanding of Marx's theory of interest it is also necessary to analyse MDC in isolation from interest-bearing capital, while recognising that the two are intimately connected in practice. But this anticipates an understanding of interest-bearing capital, and this question will be considered later.

Money-dealing capital and the rate of interest

If it is correct to treat MDC as part of merchant's capital, then it follows that it tends to earn a rate of return equal to the normal rate of profit. Consequently, MDC has no direct influence on the formation of the rate of interest, just as neither industrial nor commercial capital influences it directly. This is a result that is in direct conflict with much of bourgeois economics and also with the immediate appearance of the matter in many instances.

For most modern monetary theory, the rate of interest is at least in part determined by the supply of and demand for money. While the supply of money is often taken to be fixed or subject to government control, the demand for money is taken to depend inversely upon the rate of interest. In so far as the functions of MDC depend upon the use of a flexible quantity of money, this quantity will vary with the rate of interest. Consequently, money-dealing capital influences the demand for money and the rate of interest directly. Marx's view is different; he argues that money-dealing capital simply earns an average rate of profit like merchant's and industrial capital. As such it has no special place in the 'money market'.

At an immediate empirical level, the activities of MDC are often treated as if they involve interest payments, most notably in the rate of interest which is paid on deposits for safekeeping and in the (higher) rate of interest which is charged upon the loan of these deposits. A number of clarifying points must be made here. First, the rate of return for MDC contingent upon the difference between these rates of interest should have a tendency to equalise the rate of profit, since capital is potentially mobile in and out of

these sectors. Why should a trader who sells on credit by
borrowing to finance the purchases of customers make a
greater profit than a cash retailer, once account is taken of
interest changes, both to trader and customer? Similarly, the
handling of money or its functions is no basis upon which a
capitalist is necessarily able to earn interest. Consequently,
MDC has nothing to do with the determination of the rate of
interest (and at a complex level this is itself seen to be
ambiguous since there are different *rates* of interest, for
borrowing and lending, for example). Indeed, the rates of
interest have been taken to be exogenous; they have not
been analysed.

Second, the circumstances in which the normal rate of
profit on MDC becomes confused with interest payments
tend to be those in which MDC becomes a part of banking
capital rather than a specialised sphere of merchant's activity. It is just because banks undertake credit operations
that involve interest payments *and* also operate MDC in
which payments take the *form* of interest, that the illusion is
created that money dealing is synonymous with credit transactions. In other words, whether in conjunction with other
banking operations or not, MDC, as a portion of merchant's
capital, appears to be a portion of interest-bearing capital.
But the latter also remains to be analysed.

Interest-bearing capital

Marx's theory of interest-bearing capital (IBC) is based
upon the role of money as capital. As such, it concerns only
the borrowing and lending which takes place between the
money capitalist and other (industrial or merchant) capitalists. As such, capital becomes a commodity *sui generis* which
provides the use-value of self-expansion both for lender and
borrower, the former realising the rate of interest and the
latter the profit of enterprise which remains from the surplus
value appropriated, through the use of the money capital,
after the payment of interest. Moreover, Marx emphasises
that the price of this unique commodity is 'irrational', since
the level of the rate of interest bears no relation to any

underlying production conditions. It depends upon the competitive relations governing the classes of borrowers and lenders.

It follows that to be able to use IBC is to be able to be a capitalist rather than simply to be able to borrow. Consequently, it is not the payment of an interest as such which characterises IBC, but the use to which the loan is put. It must be advanced as money capital to embark upon a circuit of industrial capital. As it were, Marx strips aside all other credit relations and examines those between two fractions of the capitalist class, a division of the class of capitalists which produces a division of surplus value into interest and profit of enterprise. The fraction of capitalists which appropriates profit of enterprise is responsible for the functioning of capital over the industrial circuit – supervising production and sale. The fraction which appropriates interest functions as the owner of (money) capital, but it is important to recognise that this does not necessarily correspond to ownership itself. For the control of IBC is derived from the centralisation of the hoards of money which are temporarily idle in the hands of their owners but which are rendered active through the banking system. In a sense, the function of ownership of money is embodied in IBC on behalf of society as a whole, irrespective of the distribution of ownership of the individual deposits that have gone to make up the money that is subsequently loaned.

In other words, IBC arises out of two factors. The first is the formation of hoards of temporarily idle money (which are supplemented by the accumulation of capital through the surplus value realised during the sale of commodity capital). In this respect, money stands apart from the mass of commodities and represents value in its purest form. Second, money as such represents potential capital, the ability to renew and expand production of surplus value. Here there is a contrast between merchant's, including money-dealing, capital – for which the use of money is through its continuous intervention within the process of circulation, as most notably represented by its formula, $M-C-M'$ – and IBC, whose formula is $M-M'$, where money stands apart from the circulation and production of commodities.

Despite this, IBC has the closest of relations to capital accumulated in production. It is the analysis of these relations in their pure form which permits Marx to clarify certain aspects of the financial system.

First, access to IBC is a mechanism of competition between industrial capitalists. This is a constant theme throughout the three volumes of *Capital*. Increase in size of capital is the means of competitive accumulation in the pursuit of productivity increases through the introduction of machinery, and expanding use of raw materials at the relative expense of living labour.

Second, the operation of IBC does not guarantee for itself an associated 'natural' rate of interest. What must be recognised is the structural separation between control of money capital and control of productive capital. But their form of integration and the resulting division of surplus value between the two fractions is not thereby quantitatively determined. It would be quite exceptional for the rate of interest to be driven so low that it merely represented a normal rate of profit on the banker's own capital advanced. For this would require that competition within the fraction of IBC be as intense as across the sectors of industrial capital. But while competition between industrial capitals is, in part, fought by access to greater quantities of IBC, there are limitations on the extent to which this can occur within the banking sector itself. For the sector would be making loans to finance a potential rival, rather than to increase its own 'productivity', and this would have to result in the complete ineffectiveness of the control of society's idle money capital in the appropriation of surplus value.

It follows that there is competition within the IBC sector, but this is not comparable to the competitive process within the industrial sector since the potential sources of money capital for further accumulation are not systematically available through the credit system but are contingent upon relations with particular industrial capitalists and other holders of idle money. This is not to deny the tendency towards uniformity in rates of interest. Marx emphasises how quickly this is realised because of the mobility of money over the IBC sector and the uniformity of the 'commodity' involved, in contrast to the dull movement by which the rate of profit is equalised across sectors. But while uniformity is created within the sector of IBC and within the industrial sector by access to IBC, this asymmetry reflects a structural separation between the two fractions and limits the mobility between them. The result is reflected in the formation of the rate of interest, not now as a form of profit, as is the case for MDC, but as an appropriation of surplus value at the expense of profit and over and above normal profit for dealing in money, trade or industry. By the same token, this confirms the fallacy of presuming the existence of a *natural* rate of interest in parallel with a natural rate of profit. For industrial (and merchant's) capital, labour times of production (and circulation) determine the rate of profit and with it prices of production. Competition is the mechanism for establishing these. In contrast, for IBC it is competition that determines the level of the rate of interest, not only for it to be uniform within the sector itself but more fundamentally in the conflict with industrial capital over the division of surplus value between interest and profit of enterprise.

Third, and as is already clear, the existence of IBC represents a division within the capitalist class between those who monopolise the supply of IBC and those who use it as capital in production.

But, fourth, this understanding of IBC has a crucial significance for an interpretation of Marx's analysis. It is that his observations at this stage about movements in the rate of interest do not concern immediate empirical movements but rather concern those tendencies that reflect the more abstract balance between the fractions of the classes.

The logical distinctiveness of interest as an economic category

From this analysis, it emerges that there are four separate characteristics that distinguish IBC from MDC and from industrial and merchant's capital more generally. These are:

1. The use of borrowing and lending (i.e., credit relations) specifically for the purpose of advancing money capital for the appropriation of surplus value.

2. The division of surplus value into profit of enterprise
    and interest in which the latter represents a rate of
    return over and above the normal rate of profit.
3. The division of the capitalist class into two fractions.
4. The power of IBC is derived from its centralising of the
    individualised hoards of money and making them avail-
    able through the credit system as a powerful mechanism
    of competition.

Now, it is crucial that all of the conditions must hold for
the definition of interest as a separate economic category,
and this is a question of logic rather than of empirical
validity. For example, if (1) were not to hold, then IBC
would be identical to the advance of credit in general, i.e.
indistinguishable from MDC which earns the normal rate of
profit. Consequently, interest cannot be defined distinctively
even if it is used by name in practice to represent the form in
which the normal profit payments are made. The other three
conditions are necessary to guarantee the logical basis for
the distinctive category of interest, for otherwise interest
would represent the more or less temporary deviation of
the return on IBC from the normal rate of profit. This
could occur in any sector where it is favoured by market
conditions.

Marx's ability to construct a distinct theory of interest as
opposed to profit is a distinguishing mark of his economics.
In contrast to classical political economy, Marx is able to
locate interest adequately within the analytical structure of
his economic thought, thereby deriving interest as a consequence of the competitive relations between two fractions
of the capitalist class rather than as an arbitrary 'natural' rate
for which there were no determinants other than supply and
demand. Equally, within moneyless neo-classical economics, most notably for the Fisherian theory of intertemporal consumption and production, the rates of interest and
profit are conceptually identical. Even for Keynesian economics (and for Keynes himself), where monetary factors
are specifically introduced, the rate of profit – as represented by the Marginal Efficiency of Capital – is set equal to
the rate of interest. Moreover, while short-term expecta-

tions may lead to a disequilibrium value of the rate of interest, underlying Keynesianism is the idea that there is a full-employment natural or equilibrium rate of interest. This divergence from Marx's theory – and many are attracted by the idea that Keynes's liquidity theory is the complement for exchange of Marx's theory of surplus value for production – is intimately connected to Keynesian theory's failure to differentiate between demand, and hence credit, for accumulation and for consumption except for multiplier purposes.

Marx not only categorises interest distinctively, he also does so by reference to the abstract tendencies which he has identified for the capitalist economy – for the rate of profit to be equalised, for the credit system to be the mechanism of competition in accumulation, for money to stand apart from other commodities, and for idle hoards to be centralised in the banking system, etc. But because it is an analysis based on such abstract considerations, the existence and significance of interest as a category can only be determined historically and discovered by empirical analysis. Marx had much to say on these issues, but the complex material is not covered in this book.

13

Marx's Theory of Agricultural Rent

Marx's theory of rent contains two important components, a theory of differential rent and a theory of absolute rent (although there is a close connection between the two). But the basis on which he analyses rent theory is one in which private ownership of land acts as a potential obstacle to capital accumulation in the agricultural sector.

To a limited extent the same is true of orthodox rent theory (whether neo-classical or Ricardian), with private ownership usually acting through a technical constraint such as a shortage in the availability of land, either in overall supply or in supply of land of better quality, location, etc. Consequently, a rent is paid by a producer for the use of land and this emerges from the 'natural' properties of the soil (possibly interacting with the demand for its products in more sophisticated accounts).

Two interesting properties follow from this view. First, that ownership of land as such is irrelevant; ownership merely determines who is to receive the rent, not what is its level. Second, this level is determined by the given technical conditions of production (and demand).

These properties of the orthodoxy have been brought to the fore in order to bring out the major differences in Marx's approach. For him, the starting point is the existence of landed property as a specific means by which surplus value is appropriated in the form of rent. As such, rent analysis depends on a specification of the relations between landed property and capitalist production and these are, of necessity, historically specified and variable (rather than technically given).

Consequently, there can be no general theory of rent, nor can the conclusions reached in one instance be automatically applied to others. In other words, rent cannot be analysed simply on the basis of a general effect, of impeding capitalist production. For otherwise, by the same token, 'rent' would be the outcome of any obstacle to capitalist investment (and this is to some extent recognised in Marshall's notion of quasi-rents in the short run, when one capitalist has a temporarily superior method of production). Thus shortage of finance, inability to sell and a host of other conditions would have to be treated on par with rent theory, and a specific theory of the role of landed property would be irretrievably lost. In short, rent must be examined in conjunction with specific historical conditions, particularly as capitalism, as a mode of production, tends to sweep aside the barriers to its imperative to accumulate. What are the sorts of conditions characteristic of landed property which prevent that from happening?

Differential rent I

Marx's theory of differential rent (DR) is only to be understood by examining how landed property intervenes in the operation of capital within the sector of agriculture. How is it that the competitive process leaves surplus value to be appropriated in the form of rent and what are the implications of this? (In neo-classical theory, rent serves in part to allocate resources efficiently across different lands.) To confront this problem, a slight digression is needed to examine how capitals compete with each other within a sector in the absence of a significant distorting effect from land.

As argued in earlier chapters, capitals within a sector

compete with each other by raising productivity through increases in the organic composition of capital. This does not occur evenly across the sector all at the same time, so that there will be a range of individual values within the sector. Marx argues that the value of the commodity is formed out of these individual values, possibly close to the average labour time.

In the formation of the market value, excess or surplus profits will accrue to those individual capitals whose individual value is below the market value. Significantly, Marx does not insist that the market value always equals the average value. If either the most favourable or the least favourable technique is sufficiently weighty as compared with the average, then the technique concerned rather than the average regulates the sector's market value.

So within each sector of the economy there will be a range of individual values, with the lower of these gaining surplus profits when the commodity exchanges at its (usually higher) market value. The existence of these differences of profitability within the sector are a necessary condition for the existence of DR, but they are not sufficient. For otherwise, rents would exist in every sector of the economy, just as surplus profits do. Nor are natural conditions of differential productivity the source of rent or even surplus profits. They may be a condition for productivity differences, but they do not thereby create either the categories of surplus profit or rent. These depend upon the utilisation of natural conditions under capitalist relations of production and respectively, with the intervention of landed property. Differential rents exist, not because surplus profits exist, but because these are appropriated by the landlord rather than by the capitalist.

However, it is not sufficient that surplus profits exist to be appropriated in the form of rent, it is essential that they be fixed. For if they were not permanent the rent as the form of surplus profit would itself be eroded. Marx's analysis of surplus profits for industrial capital leads to the conclusion that they are eroded, since exceptional methods of production become general through competition between capitalists.

An immediate result is the explanation of differential rent

of the first type (DRI), which is usually associated with Ricardo's extensive margin. The differences of fertility be-tween lands are the source of surplus profits which are consolidated in the form of rent. Capital cannot flow onto lands of equal fertility, since they do not exist. Moreover, those capitals that do flow on to the better lands meet the barrier of landed property and forgo the surplus profit in the form of rent. The result is not simply the creation of rent but also a distortion in the formation of market-value. For DRI, the market value is not formed from the average or normal values, but by the worst *method* of production. This is not because the worst method is predominant, but because the intervention of landed property modifies the social forma-tion of value in agriculture.

Differential rent II

The theory of DRI can be constructed on the basis of equal applications of capital to the differing lands, since surplus profits arise, despite even capital accumulation across the sector, because of natural differences in fertility across the different lands. Marx's theory of differential rent of the second type, DRII, is still concerned with competition within the sector but focuses on the application of unequal capitals to the land.

The theory of DRII is more easily illustrated by consider-ing DRII in the pure form of unequal applications of capital to equal lands. In other words, the complexity of the coexistence of DRI and DRII is eliminated since there are no 'natural' differences in fertility. For an unlimited supply of land of equal quantity, the Ricardian theory would conclude that all land would bear no rent and that capital would be apportioned equally between lands. The result, particularly in its modern, neo-classical clothing, would depend upon the assumption of eventual decreasing re-turns to intensive investment. For increasing returns there could be no competitive equilibrium, and efficiency would require all capital to be invested intensively upon a single land.

In contrast, for Marx's theory, DRII would exist as capital investments larger than the normal were undertaken. These intensive cultivations would have to yield economies of scale in the use of capital, otherwise the capital would be divided and used on new no rent land. The result is to reduce the individual value below the market value, create surplus-profits, which are, however, appropriated in the form of rent. The outcome is the use of equal lands, in which unequal applications of capital result in rent on large-scale producers and an equalised rate of profit for capitalists irrespective of their size of capital. The paradox is that there are equal lands some of which yield rent and some of which do not. The lands are, however, not equal since they have different sizes of capital invested upon them. Landlords can then benefit from the progress of society in organising large-scale production through the credit system because of the way in which society progresses, through the temporary creation of surplus-profits.

DRII is based on the *temporary* surplus profits derived from the magnitude of capital invested rather than from the more or less *permanent* natural differences in fertility that are the basis for DRI. There is a tendency for competition between landowners to establish equal rents for equal lands, but this in turn will depend upon the competition among farmers who are in a position to make the same extra capital advance. Clearly all the surplus-profits that form the potential basis of DRII may not accrue to the landlord. Eventually they are eroded as the abnormal size of the investments concerned becomes normal, but this process, parallel to the one for industry, is blunted by the appropriation of DRII. Within agriculture itself, the less the incentive to the farmer to invest intensively rather than extensively, the higher DRII eats into surplus profits.

Thus, whilst agriculture may not resist absolutely the capitalist form of development, it exhibits a slow pace of progress relative to industry. This is perhaps the most important conclusion to be drawn from Marx's theory of DRII, its preoccupation with obstacles to the development of capital accumulation rather than the static formulation of the distribution of surplus value in the form of rent.

Marx's discussion of DRII in Volume III of *Capital* never undertakes an analysis of the type laid out here. DRII is not examined in the pure form of unequal applications of capital to equal lands. Marx always discusses DRII in the presence of DRI – that is, of lands of unequal quality. His reason for doing so was to analyse the quantitative determination of DRII having laid down the qualitative basis for its existence. If DRI and DRII were independent of each other, the analysis of DR would now be complete, for then DRI would have the effect of equalising lands so that DRII could be calculated from the profitability of surplus capital. Alternatively, DRII would have the effect of equalising the effects of different applications of capital so that DRI could be calculted from the differing fertilities between lands. In effect, DR is the simple addition of DRI and DRII.

This procedure is, however, invalid. DRI and DRII have each been calculated on the basis of certain abstractions concerning the distribution of capitals and fertilities. There is no presumption that the interaction of DRI and DRII is simply additive. A more complex analysis is necessarily involved concerning the coexistence of unequal lands and unequal capitals on those lands. For DRI, there is the problem of determining the worst land in the presence of unequal applications of capital (DRII). Some lands may be worst for one level of investment but not for others, for example. Second, for DRII, there is the problem of determining the normal level of investment in the presence of differing lands (DRI). Some capitals may be normal for some types of lands, other capitals normal for other lands. There is a further difficulty for DRII, since decreasing productivity of additional investments would not allow for surplus profits for abnormally large capitals unless the market value of the agriculture product rises. This raises the question of whether the market value should be determined by the individual value on some plot of land or whether it may be determined by some part of capital on that land. In other words, is the size of normal capital always the total capital applied to some land, or can it be some part of that

capital? Even the term 'normal capital' becomes inappropriate, for the capital's application to a particular land to
determine market value is in no sense general.

These problems concern the simultaneous determination
of worst land and normal capital in agriculture. The interaction of the two gives rise to market value from which
differential rents can be calculated. For industrial capital,
the determination of normal capital is synonymous with the
determination of value. The problem does not arise. The
same is true for each of DRI and DRII in the absence of the
other. For DRI in its pure form (equal capitals), the determination of worst land is synonymous with the determination of value, whereas for DRII in its pure form (equal
lands) it is the determination of normal capital that comes to
the fore in the determination of value.

This problem of the joint determination of normal capital
and worst land (or, more exactly, normal land, since the
physically worst land in use may not be the one to determine
value) cannot be determined abstractly. As discussed previously, it will depend upon historically contingent conditions, on how agriculture has developed in the past and
how it continues to relate to capital accumulation as broadly
understood in terms of capitalists' access to the land (which
may be affected by legal, financial and other sorts of
conditions). In short, DR theory does not produce a deter-
minate analysis of rent but reveals the processes by which it
might be historically examined.

Absolute rent

If the key to the formation of differential rent is the
establishment of market value and surplus-profit through
competition *within* the agricultural sector, the basis for the
formation of absolute rent (AR) is to be found in the surplus
profits that exist in the transformation from market values to
prices of production. In these items, AR can be seen to have
DR as its point of departure. Both concern the obstacle to
capital investment posed by landed property and the associated appropriation of surplus profit in the form of rent, but

each is located at a different level of analysis and therefore has a different source of surplus. DR depends upon the divergence between individual and market values, AR on the divergence between market values and prices of production.

This basis for the formation of AR has been confused with a condition for its existence, the flow of capital on to new lands. The formation of prices of production depends upon the flow of capital between sectors. The flow into agriculture is obstructed by the existence of landed property. If this flow were, despite the barrier, to be located on existing lands in use, then the principles of differential rent would apply. AR depends then upon the flow of capital *on to new lands*.

In purely technical terms, Marx's theory of AR is as follows. Because agriculture has a lower organic composition of capital than industry it produces additional surplus value because of the higher proportion of living labour employed. Consequently, in the absence of landed property, its price of production would be below value. However, landed property makes an intervention that prevents the formation of price of production in agriculture, and agricultural commodities sell at a price above price of production and in the limit at value, the difference from price of production making up AR. In addition, the conditions in which AR would disappear are (a) if the composition of capital in agriculture were equal to or higher than average, or (b) if all land had been taken into cultivation, i.e. AR depends upon the movement on to new lands; (c) if the level of development of agriculture were equal to that of industry.

If, however, we restrict the interpretation of Marx's theory of AR to technical considerations alone, then it is liable to be a static theory of surplus value distribution. In this, landlords gain a rent because they can prevent the flow of capital into a sector. This however, is, AR as a monopoly rent. Similar considerations would apply in the complete absence of landed property – if, there were an essential patent involved in the production process. There are other problems, for Marx's conditions for the existence of AR become purely arbitrary. This is true of the dependence of AR on low OCC in agriculture, particularly when it is recognised that OCCs differ within industry without rent being formed. Leaving this objection aside, there would be no reason for AR to be limited to the difference between value and price of production. As a monopoly rent, the market price could rise above the value according to the ability and willingness of industry to pay and landowners not to compete.

However, Marx's discussion of the conditions under which AR would disappear suggest that a static theory is not involved. It is the pace of development of agriculture relative to industry and the movement of capital on to new lands that is of importance. Of course, these conditions can be interpreted statically (all land is leased, all sectors have equal levels of development), but if they are not then the other concepts utilised, in particular the OCC, must themselves be interpreted in a dynamic context relative to Marx's theory of accumulation. In understanding this task, it will be shown that Marx's theory of AR is correct in all essential respects and does not require modification or rejection to be consistent with his analysis of capital.

Suppose initially that the OCC is equal across all industries and given by c relative to v, and that the OCC in industry and potentially in agriculture can be increased by a proportion $b > 1$ (so that given labour now converts bc constant capital into final goods rather than c). For agriculture, value minus price of production

$$= c + v + ev - (c + v)(1 + r), \quad \text{where } r \text{ is the rate of profit and } e \text{ the rate of exploitation}$$

$$= ev - (c + v)r$$

$$= ev - \frac{(c + v)ev}{bc + v} \text{ since } r = \frac{ev}{bc + v}$$

$$= \frac{ev}{bc + v}(bc + v - c - v)$$

$$= rc(b - 1).$$

But $rc(b - 1)$ is precisely the surplus profits arising out of the increasing OCC, since it is the rate of profit multiplied by the additional constant capital set in motion. These surplus profits correspond to the DRII which would be charged if the OCC were increased on existing lands in use. It follows that AR is limited by the difference between value and price of production in correspondence to the upper limit on the charge for extensive cultivation posed by the alternative application of capital to intensive cultivation (DRII).

In the light of this understanding of AR, it is possible to reinterpret the conditions in which it would disappear. Once the OCC in agriculture has developed to the same level as industry, the obstacle posed by DRII to intensive cultivation must have been eroded. This condition is equivalent to the equal development of agriculture and industry given a correct interpretation of the OCC. It is a sufficient but not necessary condition for the disappearance of AR, because it also requires the erosion of the effects of DRII as an obstacle to capital accumulation. On the other hand, if all land were leased, cultivation would have to progress intensively, but not necessarily efficiently, and the obstacle posed by landed property would be formed.

We have shown that the movement on to new land, the relative underdevelopment of agriculture, and a low OCC in agriculture are all conditions for the existence of AR. None is a cause of its existence. Rather, all are the result of the obstacle to capital accumulation posed by landed property as capital moves between sectors of the economy, creating surplus profits in agriculture that are then appropriated as rent.

Conclusion

It has been shown that Marx's theory of rent is a coherent extension of his theory of capital to accumulation confronting the barrier of landed property. Differential rent has been seen to depend upon the existence of surplus profits formed through competition within the agricultural sector. DRI results from the divergence of individual values from market values due to 'natural' conditions, DRII from the divergence due to unequal applications of capital. AR is shown to arise from the existence of surplus profits on the basis of competition between capitals of different sectors.

Rent depends upon the production and appropriation of surplus value through the intervention of landed property. It draws upon the theory of production, the theory of accumulation, the theory of the formation of value and the theory of prices of production. As such, it is probably the most complex application of Marx's abstract understanding of the capitalist economy. At the same time, it clearly reveals its own limits in showing how further analysis is contingent upon exactly how landed property has developed and interacted with capitalist development.

14

Concluding Remarks

As remarked in the Preface to the second edition, this book was and is very much a product of its times. Now times have changed. Following the student radicalism of the 1960s, interest in and the development of Marxism blossomed. It did so in favourable circumstances, as the post-war boom in the economy, and in the education sector, had yet to come to a close. As a result, the understanding and status of Marxist economics reached a relatively high level. This was particularly important as, within the social sciences, Marxism has always had a lower status in economics, whereas in others it has more frequently been seen at least as an important potential alternative and not simply to be ignored.

Since the mid-1970s, there have continued to be substantial contributions to the development of Marxist economics, despite a less favourable external environment. But the more general commitment to and popularity of Marxist economics has suffered. Fewer university teachers are able or willing to offer Marxist economics as an option, let alone as a core course. Ironically, as the demands placed upon economics have expanded in terms of explaining, for example, persistent high levels of unemployment, so it has become more esoteric and removed from the everyday realities of economic life (as most sharply illustrated by the role of rational expectations as an important explanatory factor, and not just in the new classical economics). Just when Marxist economics seems most appropriate for exploring the continuing contradictions of capitalist society, academia is at its most neglectful of it.

There have been other developments, too, which mean that the low status of Marxist economics has not simply been restored as before. The challenge previously posed by Marxist economics has led to a response in which propositions associated with Marx have been integrated into orthodox models. Thus, where it does continue, much academic Marxist economics has revolved around mathematical models in which fixed technology and equilibrium pricing, for example, have assumed a prominent role.

This is not necessarily to be regretted, since Marxist economics can only prosper by being exposed to competing interpretations and developments. However, the result has often been that many confronting Marxist economics for the first, and possibly the only, time will be given a false representation of Marx's own economics. For whilst some writers are careful to recognise how they depart from Marx's own intentions, others are less scholarly and present, as a formalisation of Marx's economics, analysis which is entirely inconsistent with it.

In this respect, even if differently, the status quo has been restored in so far as the Marxist economics commonly made available diverges from Marx's own economics. Previously, there had been a tendency to (mis)represent Marx superficially and thereby dismiss his contribution relatively easily. With this revised edition of *Marx's 'Capital'* I hope to have helped those studying Marxist economics not to fall into such traps and to sustain the tradition of Marxist economics that is true to Marx.

Index